Teaching Your Child About God

You Can't Begin Too Soon

Wes Haystead

A Division of G/L Publications
Ventura, CA U.S.A.

The foreign language publishing of all Regal books is under the direction of GLINT. GLINT provides financial and technical help for the adaptation, translation and publishing of books in more than 85 languages for millions of people worlwide. For information regarding translation, contact: GLINT,P.O. Box 6688, Ventura, California 93006.

Cloth Edition, 1981

Published by Regal Books
A Division of GL Publications
Ventura, California 93006
Printed in the U.S.A.

Library of Congress Cataloging in Publication Data

Haystead, Wesley.
Teaching your child about God.

Previously published as: You can't begin too soon. Glendale, Calif.: International Center for Learning, 1974.
Bibliography: p.
1. Christian education of preschool children.
2. Children—Religious life. I. Title.
BV1475.8.H383 1981 649'.7 81-13842
ISBN 0-8307-0798-0 AACR2

For the sake of easier reading, the use of the pronouns, *he, him* and *his* in this publication refer for the most part to both male and female in the generic sense.

Contents

CHAPTER ONE

The Child and Christian Concepts

"Is this God's house?"
"Yes, Randy, it is."
"Then, where's His bedroom?"

"Where is God?"
"Well, Karen, God is everywhere."
(Thoughtful silence). "But I can't see Him."
"That's because He is a spirit. He doesn't have a body. He's invisible."
(More silence). "Is He in this room?"
"Yes, He's always with us wherever we go."
"Is He under my chair?" (Giggle.)
"What if I step on Him?" (More giggles.)

"God is rich, isn't He, Teacher?"

"Why do you think so, David?"

" 'Cause my Mom and Dad give Him lots of money in church." (No comment.) "But Jesus is poor."

"Why is that?"

" 'Cause He only gets the pennies I bring to Sunday School."

Each parent or teacher has his own favorite collection of humorous things young children say. We try to suppress our merriment at the moment, but then rush off to regale other adults with the "cute thing little Harry said this morning."

Perhaps these childish interpretations are not really funny at all. Is it possible that early misconceptions will stay with a child as he grows, distorting understandings and attitudes, making him resistive to more mature knowledge? Will these initial ideas of God go the same route as Santa Claus, the Easter Bunny, and the Tooth Fairy? Can a four-year-old, who thinks of God as an old man with a white beard sitting on a cloud, have his spiritual development delayed or warped by this non-biblical image? To answer this question, we need first to consider the basic nature of a young child and how he thinks. For the child will use the same processes in attempting to understand spiritual concepts that he uses to grapple with any other part of his fascinating and ever-expanding world.

THE NATURE OF CHILDREN

Each child is a total person. Every part of his nature interacts powerfully on every other part. His mental, emotional, physical, social and spiritual processes are so tightly intermingled as to be literally inseparable.

For example, a child's simple physical movements also have powerful emotional importance for him. Succeeding at dressing himself unassisted carries strong feelings of accomplishment which dramatically affect the child's attitude about himself. Each experience in the child's life touches not just one, but several dimensions of his personality.[1]

When adults understand that a child functions as a total entity, efforts to teach him at any level require that they understand the complete child. They must also understand that a child's attitude also affects his learning. How he feels about a learning situation greatly affects the success or failure of his efforts.

The developmental process

Perhaps the most striking aspect of the child's nature is how quickly he changes. This continuous growth process involves several important concepts.

First, the child's capacities for acquiring skills, handling his emotions and developing understandings depend upon the satisfaction of basic physical and psychological needs. For instance, adequate nutrition is essential for healthy growth in all areas. Mastery of any material depends on feelings of security. Feelings of confidence and self-worth grow out of the many experiences of daily living in which a child succeeds in achieving a goal. Recognition of these facts helps adults avoid pushing young children too fast. Early childhood is primarily a time for nurturing a healthy body and building strong feelings of security and personal value. Neither can be rushed. And neither can be easily rebuilt once the early years of life are past.[2,3]

The second principle of growth is closely related to the first. Early childhood experiences, both positive and negative, live on to powerfully influence the child, the youth, and even the adult. These early years have awesome significance for later maturity.[4]

Third, the child's growth can be observed in terms of recognizable stages. Physically, the child passes through stages of lying, sitting, crawling, standing, walking and finally running. Socially, his play starts out as solitary, then includes another child as a companion to a parallel activity, grows to become interactive with one or more children. Finally play becomes truly cooperative with others. Mentally, the child's thought is limited to his senses and movements, gradually enlarges to deal with reality, and finally in adolescence becomes capable of abstract reason.[5] There are no clear lines between one stage of development and the next. However, the main characteristics are visible. Adults need to understand what behavior is typical of a child at any particular stage of development.[6]

A child's growth and development pattern is not an inclined plane, gently and continuously rising. It is, rather, a series of hills and valleys, ups and downs, yet generally moving forward. A child's growth process is uneven. He may develop rapidly in one area and slowly in another. The rate of growth in any one area will vary from time to time. Yet, because the child functions as a total entity, growth in any area affects every other area of his personality. The interrelationships, however, are highly complex, and adults should be alert to a child's total growth patterns, not just the development in one or two areas.

Finally, the child's development is profoundly affected by his interaction with the people around him. Relationships with the grown-ups and children in his life are foundational to the child's growing view of himself and his world. The way he perceives other people's reactions to himself greatly influences his total growth pattern.

HOW A CHILD THINKS

The infant appears on the scene with no awareness of the heritage of human knowledge. As far as that new eight-pound-seven-ounce tax exemption is concerned, Newton never explained gravity, Edison never harnessed electricity, and Armstrong never set foot on the moon. He doesn't even know there is a moon! All the little fellow arrives with is the basic equipment that will make him capable of discovering these things. And he starts working at that task from the moment he emerges from his crowded, but comfortable, womb.

Thinking depends on experiences

Despite efforts of cartoonists to occasionally depict the newborn as capable of adult-type thought and reaction, a baby's thought patterns are vastly different from those of grown-ups. For example, during the first year of life, the child does not recognize the existence of objects unless he can see them. Demonstrate this fact by letting a baby focus on an object; then cover it from his view. The infant will act as though the object never existed. As the months pass, he may gradually begin to show signs of distress when the object is hidden. However, it is usually not until the first half of his second year that he will begin searching to locate the object. He must have considerable experience with objects before he is able to think about the object when it is not present.[7]

Even when the child is able to distinguish object permanency, he remains limited in his ability to effectively think of himself as separate from his surroundings. A long process of exploring, manipulating, handling and looking is necessary for the young child to conclude that physically, he is a separate individual. Toward the end of his second year and throughout the third, he works hard at developing a psychological identity. The well-known negativism of a two-year-old is the means by which he seeks to work out a view of himself as capable of making decisions. His sense of autonomy is not the result of careful reasoning. He develops it from many repeated encounters with his environment.[8]

Thinking is limited by perspective

A child's early years are marked by his inability to recognize another person's point of view. He assumes that everyone sees and experiences things in the same way he does.[9] This limited perspective involves more than simply a visual viewpoint. No one was more startled than one-year-old Billy when little Janie screamed because he pinched her. When he felt no pain as a result of his action, why should she? A child begins life unable to conceive that anything happened or existed before he was born. Five-year-old Karen was very startled one afternoon in McDonald's restaurant to realize that not everyone there knew who she was.

This outlook on life, so powerfully limited by the child's desires, causes great difficulty in understanding concepts relating to the Christian faith. Since a child has nothing else with which to work, he uses pieces of his own surroundings to formulate an idea of what God is like. This idea is one that fits his own expectations and experiences. This child-manufactured concept often has no real relationship or resemblance to the God revealed to us in the Bible.

Also, since the child tends to endow inanimate objects with feelings and desires similar to his own, he often treats his idea of God the same way. God becomes the child's greatest dream fulfiller. Until the child has had many and varied opportunities for firsthand experiences to recognize that different viewpoints exist, he has no alternative than to assume his explanation is correct.[10]

Another characteristic of a young child's thinking is his tendency to focus attention on limited or nonessential aspects of a situation.[11] In the same manner as the famous cat who went to London and was impressed only by the mouse under the queen's chair, the child sees only those things which have meaning to him, regardless of their significance. To demonstrate, show two transparent jars of different shape and size to a young child. Put water in one jar. Then pour that water into the other jar. Ask him if there is more or less water in the second jar. At first most children under six conclude that the quantity of water has changed, since the container is either taller or shorter. The new shape of the liquid obscures the seemingly obvious fact that the amount of water did not change.

This characteristic of a child's thought process has been observed often in children's reactions to Bible stories. Bobby sat wide-eyed listening to his mother tell him the Christmas story. At the conclusion, he wondered if there had been any angels singing when he was born. He resolved his own question by deciding angels could not have been there "because there weren't any shepherds around." In Bobby's thinking the uniqueness of the birth of Jesus depended on the strange occurrences. The actual significance totally eluded him because he fastened his attention on parts of the story that were for him important, but were actually only secondary aspects.

Related to his inability to focus on the significance of a situation is the ease with which a child can give correct answers that are in fact meaningless to him. Since his vocabulary starts at zero and virtually explodes during these first six years, he continually encounters words and ideas that are completely beyond his comprehension. Often the child's lack of word meanings will betray him. One day Alice solemnly prayed for "all the missionaries working in the corn fields." The idea of a "foreign field" was totally beyond her understanding, so she naturally rephrased her prayer in a way that made sense to her.

Many times, however, the child is able to produce the answer expected by adults. He then receives praise for his performance and goes about his business, although both he and the adults are unaware that what he said was meaningless to him. Thus, misunderstanding is often allowed to continue with no one aware of its presence.

Thinking is limited to physical activities

Beside the limitations of this restricted perspective, the child's mental development requires physical objects to manipulate. Concrete experiences form the basic structure of early childhood thinking. Five-year-old Marie was puzzled for a long time about clouds. She had flown through them in an airplane and observed them in many different formations. However, she was bothered by not knowing what they really were and how rain came from them. Her parents soon realized that verbal explanations of evaporation and condensation offered little help. One day Marie noticed steam rising from a hot cup of coffee. "That looks like a cloud." At last the door was open to her beginning comprehension of the marvels of clouds, thanks to exposure to a physical experience.

Abstract ideas must be recast in physical terms for the child to attach meaning to them. The little girl who talks of her love for Mommy and Daddy knows nothing of an abstract quality labeled "love," but only of the hugs and kisses and feelings of well-being she receives from her parents.

Concepts relating to the Christian faith, many of which deal with the least physical ideas man is capable of conceiving, are visualized by young children in physical terms. For the child, God is a man, greater than ordinary men in highly significant ways, but still a man. He resides in a specific place and has feelings and reactions, as well as a body, in common with men. Five-year-old Lynn was asked, "If God weren't a man, what else could He be?" After giving the question ample thought, she concluded logically, "He'd have to be a little children." Since thinking of God as an animal was repugnant to Lynn, she simply concluded God must be another size human being.

How thinking grows

A major factor in a child's thought maturation process is the quality and quantity of his firsthand experiences. For example, after Davey enountered his neighbor's dog on several occasions, he proceeded to label any four-legged animal as a "bow-wow." The fact that some of these creatures uttered "meow," "moo," and "baa," gradually brought him to recognize the distinctions. He learned animal categories by a combination of exposure to the animals and their sounds; also by the patient guidance of his parents while looking at picture books. His maturation is a continuing process of adjusting ideas in the light of new experiences. However, if there are no new experiences in a certain area of learning, the adjustments may be a long time in coming.

A four-year-old boy who watched a deliveryman bring a large bottle of water to his house every week was heard to repeat the Twenty-third Psalm as, " . . . He leadeth me beside distilled water." His version was the result of his lack of firsthand experience with a pool of quiet water suitable for sheep to drink. Since he was unable to grasp the original intent of the statement, he forged his misconception from an event that was within his firsthand experience.

Parents and teachers must realize the young child's dependence on experience to insure effective learning. In his Christian education particularly, he needs a variety of opportunities to put Christian concepts into action, to practice living what God's Word says, to give as well as receive love. Teaching that relies totally on verbal explanations is doomed to leave the young child's concepts at the mercy of his limited experience.

WHY TEACH CHRISTIAN CONCEPTS TO YOUNG CHILDREN

In light of a child's limited mental capabilities, would it not be better to postpone his Christian education until his thought process is more fully developed? Should parents and teachers even attempt to introduce children under six to ideas that baffle adults?

The Bible commands that children be taught the faith

Since Christians look to the Bible as the guidebook of their faith, the best place to seek an answer to this question is in its pages. God's Word does say some highly significant things to parents concerning their teaching responsibilities.

Exodus 12:24-27. On the fateful eve of Israel's deliverance from Egyptian slavery, Moses instructed the elders in the proper procedures for the Passover observance, not just for that single occasion, but as a permanent celebration. "And you shall observe this event as an ordinance for you and your children forever" (v. 24). The intent of the annual repetition of the ritual was to portray physically that historic event in such a way as to arouse questions among the children. Their questions were to then provide opportunity to explain the significance of the symbols.

Deuteronomy 6. Here Moses presents Israel with the essence of God's commandments, clearly stating a formula for teaching them to children. Parents are instructed to obey the commandments themselves and to make the commandments subject of conversation "when you sit in your house and when you walk by the way and when you lie down and when you rise up" (v. 7). Instruction pertaining to obedience to God was not seen as a formal presentation to passive listeners, but as a process of continually using the everyday occurrences of the child's life as a means of awakening interest in the things of the Lord.

The importance of the parents consistently doing "what is right and good in the sight of the Lord" (v. 18), reflects the powerful effect of parental example. *The emphasis is on giving the child a model to observe rather than commands to obey.* The verbal explanations are left to the child's initiative, stimulated by a consistent parental pattern of life.

Proverbs 22:6. "Start a boy on the right road, and even in old age he will not leave it" (*NEB*). The Hebrew word translated as "start" carries the idea of initiating or disciplining, which infers again a process of teaching by consistent example. The "right road," or course of life, is one that is proper and positive of itself, and fits the unique capacities of the particular child.

Proverbs 13:24. "He who spares his rod hates his son, but he who loves him disciplines him diligently." Unfortunately, some people interpret these words as an admonition to use physical punishment as the primary means of discipline.

A more accurate interpretation of this statement, as well as others on the same subject in Proverbs (3:12; 19:18; 22:15; 23:13,14; 29:15,17), suggests that physical punishment is sometimes necessary in dealing with a child. However, it must be motivated by deep love and concern for the child's welfare, never as an angry means of retaliation for a disobedient action. To diligently discipline a child is to be consistent and realistic in what behavior is expected, to seek the most effective approach to correction, and not one that simply provides satisfaction for the parent's frustrations.

Matthew 18:1-10. "See that you do not despise one of these little ones" (v. 10). Jesus warned His listeners to recognize children as valuable human beings with rights of their own. Then He concluded with a remarkable answer to the question, "Who then is greatest in the kingdom of heaven?" (v. 1). He seated a child in the middle of the group and urged His hearers to "become like children" (v. 3). Clearly He emphasized that childhood possesses qualities of great worth and inherent value that must be respected by adults.

However, His point was evidently missed by His disciples, who at a later meeting attempted to stop parents from bringing their children to Jesus (Mark 10:13-16). "When Jesus saw this, He was indignant and said to them, 'Permit the children to come to Me; do not hinder them; for the kingdom of God belongs to such as these' " (v. 14). For nearly two thousand years people have used this example of Jesus as their inspiration for efforts to introduce young lives to Christian teaching. Note what Jesus did when the children came to Him: "And He took them in His arms and began blessing them" (v. 16). No record exists that He sat them down and began lecturing them. He loved them and let them go.

Ephesians 6:4. "Fathers, do not provoke your children to anger; but bring them up in the discipline and instruction of the Lord." The negative command warns parents to evaluate their child-raising approach in terms of the child's reaction. If frustration or discouragement result, the method used was inappropriate, no matter how well intentioned. The second part of this verse is a positive exhortation that combines teaching by action (discipline) and teaching by word (instruction). The use of both these words indicates the apostle's recognition of the need for a balance between activity and spoken words.

Second Timothy 1:5; 3:15. "For I am mindful of the sincere faith within you, which first dwelt in your grandmother Lois, and your mother Eunice, and I am sure that it is in you as well . . . and that from childhood you have known the sacred writings which are able to give you the wisdom that leads to salvation through faith which is in Christ Jesus." In this brief letter, Paul makes reference to Timothy's childhood—the time when Timothy had become acquainted with the Bible. Paul commends Timothy's mother and grandmother for having provided the source of Timothy's youthful faith.

Two important facts stand out in these biblical references concerning children. First, the home is the focal point of responsibility for religious instruction. Second, the teaching is done through actions followed by words. Parental example, daily experiences and ceremonial observances are the raw material to introduce a child to concepts concerning the Lord. The picture is clearly one in which the home is urged to create a climate that prepares a child for verbal explanations.

Isolating a child from religion is impractical

"I want my child to make his own decision about his religion. I don't want to prejudice him by what I think," are the sentiments of some well-meaning parents.

It is virtually impossible to totally isolate a child from

some exposure to religious ideas. Even in non-Christian homes, a child will encounter playmates who go to Sunday School, see church buildings in his neighborhood, catch religious programs on television and radio, and hear the ubiquitous reliance on religious terms in profanity. These scattered impressions are enough to raise questions in children's minds. If a child's understanding is left to his own imagination, distorted ideas will most likely be the result.

For the child whose parents possess a deep faith in God, total avoidance of religious knowledge in the early years is even less feasible, even if those parents should desire to arrange it. Their own beliefs influence their everyday behavior in significant ways. A child's questions are sure to come. Attempts to evade answering do more harm than good. They leave the child to construct his own limited explanation and lessen the possibilities of future communication between parent and child as other questions are raised.

Ability to handle difficult concepts comes through experience

Since a child learns through his experiences, the absence of religious instruction during the early years of his life would tend to retard his spiritual and emotional growth. No one seriously advocates insulating a child from all letters and books before he is old enough to read. Nor is experimentation with writing implements withheld until the child is ready to write legibly. Experimenting and practice are necessary parts of the learning process. Why should learning about Christian concepts be regarded any differently? Why not give the child many firsthand experiences that encourage his spiritual growth and broaden his understanding of the Christian faith?

Christian teaching helps meet needs of young children

Early childhood education is receiving more attention today than ever before from educators, parents and even politicians. This mushrooming interest which began in the 1960s results from a fervent hope that positive experiences in the first years of life will lay a solid foundation for later achievement and success. There has been a substantial accumulation of evidence that early learning plays a vital role in all areas of a child's development. A primary factor is the importance of helping the young child learn how to learn. Successes in early learning have shown positive results in developing healthy expectations for later experiences, while early failures diminish the child's belief in his ability to achieve.[12] In Christian education, positive feelings about the people, places and ideas associated with the learning experiences are very important in preparing a child for later instruction. The child who has had pleasant experiences with people who talk to him about God will be far more open to learning new concepts than one whose experiences have been unhappy.

Some parents and teachers are so concerned about the child's future that his present learning needs are often overlooked. Linda's mother was deeply concerned that her four-year-old grow up with solid biblical knowledge. She surrounded Linda with Bible storybooks and began drilling her in memorizing Bible verses. She knew that

Linda's understanding of much of the material was very limited, but she felt convinced that learning it now would somehow be helpful later on. Unfortunately, Linda's mother did not realize that a child's retention of things with little meaning or present usefulness is very low. Even though Linda enjoyed the attention she got from her mother while learning this material, she actually began to develop feelings that things pertaining to the Bible were not practical or related to her current experience.

Can Christian education effectively meet any of the present needs of a young child? Linda's mother could more appropriately have met her daughter's four-year-old needs by using a few stories and verses that referred to actions and feelings that were familiar to Linda. Then, whenever Linda encountered a situation similar to a verse or story, Mother could make effective reference to it. (See chapter 5 for positive suggestions in using the Bible with young children.)

While relating Bible content to the child's life is very helpful, the living of Bible truths by adults is the most significant way in which a young child's needs are met. When a parent's faith makes that parent feel secure and able to give love, then the whole environment of the child is enriched. The child's essential needs will be more adequately met as Dad and Mom find strength and encouragement in coping with life's frustrations. A child's early environment has great significance in shaping his basic personality and his attitude toward learning.

Recognition of this fact points out the absolute necessity of parents giving first attention to their own spiritual health. Tensions for the child result when a parent declares one thing but lives another. A pattern of inconsistency created real problems for Allen. His father read from the Bible about God's love for people. But the father rarely showed any affection for Allen, who thus had no adequate model to use as a reference in establishing his idea of God. Allen's father never learned to apply a biblical truth to daily living, and passed that failing on to his son.

The child under six has some personal needs which knowing Bible truths helps to satisfy. He needs to see a sense of order in his physical surroundings. He needs to feel that his own life and his world of family, home and friends are all part of God's loving plan. If the young child can early believe in and count on God's unconditional love for him as a person of great worth, he can begin to cope with the experiences of living in today's world in the security of His unchanging love. And this confidence in God's dependability is a reflection of one's learning that God can be trusted.

A child's need for love is also satisfied by assurance that God does love him. This knowledge is highly meaningful for the child who is surrounded by love at home. Or, it can be a light in the darkness for the child who feels rejected. However, the idea of God's love will carry meaning only to the degree the child has received real love from an understanding adult who has himself experienced God's love.

When the child is secure in his feelings of being loved, he can develop feelings of self-esteem. Christian teachings can contribute here, too, as the child learns to see himself as important to God, an individual with unique capacities and worth. By the time the child turns six he has developed firm opinions about himself. In many little ways he shows that he feels good about who he is, or that he finds coping with challenges beyond him. This attitude will color all his experiences and relationships, powerfully molding the kind of person he becomes.

His experiences with Christian concepts play an important part in formulating his basic self-concept. Specific facts or stories have little impact compared to the contribution of experiences and relationships that he associates with those concepts.

Investigators into the significance of attitudes in the relationship between young children and Christian teaching have compared the child's feelings toward his parents with his feelings toward God. The similarities in these attitudes are striking. The feelings toward God are warmest when the child feels very positively toward both parents. The conclusions of these studies show that parental influence is extremely potent in shaping a child's attitude toward God. There is no substitute for a good relationship if teaching is to be effective with young children. The relationship between parent and child seems to overpower whatever factual knowledge the child might possess.

Parents who want to help their children grow toward a mature understanding of the Christian faith need to begin by building a warm, open relationship with the child when he is young. Parents can build a solid foundation for a child's Christian growth when they help that child know he is loved and respected. On the other hand, all the lectures and instructions in the world will have little impact if a positive parent-child relationship does not exist.

Notes

1. Dorothy C. Briggs, *Your Child's Self-Esteem: The Key to His Life* (Garden City, N.Y.: Doubleday, 1970), p.3.
2. Erik Erikson, *Childhood and Society*, 2nd ed. (New York: Norton, 1963), p. 247 ff.
3. A. H. Maslow, *Motivation and Personality* (New York: Harper & Row, 1954).
4. Jean Piaget, *Science of Education and the Psychology of the Child* (New York: Orion, 1970), p. 127.
5. Ibid., p. 36.
6. Donna Harrell and Wesley Haystead, *Creative Bible Learning for Young Children* (Ventura: Regal Books, 1977), pp. 33-67.
7. H. Munsinger, *Fundamentals of Child Development* (New York: Rinehart & Winston, 1971), pp. 268-275.
8. J. D. Navarra, *The Development of Scientific Concepts in a Young Child* (New York: Columbia University, 1955), p. 85.
9. David Elkind, "Development of Religious Ideas in Children," in *Research on Religious Development*, M. P. Stromment, Ed. (New York: Hawthorn, 1971), p. 52.
10. Piaget, *Child's Conception of the World*, p. 376.
11. Ronald Goldman, *Religious Thinking from Childhood to Adolescence* (New York: Seabury, 1964), p. 52.
12. Lawrence J. Schweinhart and David P. Weikart, "Research Report—Can Preschool Education Make a Lasting Difference?" in *Bulletin of the High/Scope Foundation* (Ypsilanti, MI), Fall 1977, pp. 1-5.

CHAPTER TWO

The Child and Self

"What's your name?"

"Bobby."

"Is that all of your name, or is there more?"

"I think my whole name is Bobby Stop It!"

This active little fellow had evidently driven his harried mother into numerous utterances of what seemed to him to be his full identification. During the hectic process of rapid growth in the early years of life, children acquire many labels, both verbal and nonverbal.

"He's all boy! What a handful!"

"She's such a pretty little doll."

"He just never sits still. I don't know what I'm going to do with him."

"Oh, what a good boy you are! You ate all your peas!"

"Why are you so naughty? That was a bad, bad thing!"

The list of statements and attitudes that people convey to young children in response to their behavior is endless. From infancy, almost every move the child makes seems to elicit some reactions from parents. These reactions have a powerful impact on the child. By accumulating all the bits and pieces of encounters with other people, he begins his lifelong task of building his self-image. He gradually and continually discovers what kind of person he is.[1]

Thus, the child who is consistently told he is clumsy and uncoordinated, who hears a constant stream of "Be careful . . . watch out! You'll spill it . . . no, you're too little. Let Daddy do it . . . see, I told you you couldn't carry that!" naturally concludes from such overwhelming evidence that he is indeed clumsy. He therefore becomes far more likely to drop things, for example, since he lacks the confidence to achieve success.

The feelings the child has about himself, created through repeated encounters with people and things, loom very large in determining how the child will respond to his world.[2] This self-image permeates the thoughts and behavior of the child, coloring all his relationships, including his ideas of God.

Jennie was a first-time visitor to Sunday School. The teachers expected her to be shy. However, as the morning wore on, she continued to remain withdrawn from the activities and from the other children. Mr. Harrison attempted to involve her in conversation. After trying several topics with no success, he was rather surprised when Jennie firmly declared, "I don't like Sunday School." Thinking this statement was simply the result of being in unfamiliar surroundings, Mr. Harrison assured Jennie that he understood her fearful feelings. But Jennie persisted, "I don't like Sunday School because I don't like God."

"Do you want to tell me why you don't like God?" asked Mr. Harrison.

"Because I'm ugly," was Jennie's reply.

All of her five-year-old life Jennie had been unfavorably compared with her older sister in appearance, ability and eventually, disposition. Feeling unlovely and unloved, she directed her resentment at a God who "made me ugly." She, of course, was unable to realize that it was her parents' insensitive lack of appreciation for individual differences that was the source of her unhappiness.

WHAT THE BIBLE SAYS ABOUT SELF-IMAGE

Scripture consistently depicts behavior as resulting from the thought patterns of the individual.

"Oh that they had such a heart in them, that they would fear Me, and keep My commandments always" (Deut. 5:29).

"Give to my son Solomon a perfect heart to keep Thy commandments, Thy testimonies, and Thy statutes, and to do them all" (1 Chron. 29:19).

"As he thinks within himself, so he is" (Prov. 23:7).

There are also frequent exhortations for men to be realistic in their self-appraisals: "I say to every man among you not to think more highly of himself than he ought to think; but to think so as to have sound judgment" (Rom. 12:3). "Let no one keep defrauding you of your prize by delighting in self-abasement" (Col. 2:18). Between these extremes is the concept of humility, which the Lord Jesus made the cornerstone of Christian character. In the Jewish literature, humility had traditionally been considered a positive virtue. "But the humble will inherit the land, and will delight themselves in abundant prosperity. . . . And [if] My people who are called by My name humble themselves and pray, seek My face and turn from their wicked ways, then I will hear from heaven, will forgive their sin, and will heal their land. . . . The fear of the Lord is the instruction for wisdom, and before honor comes humility" (Ps. 37:11; 2 Chron. 7:14; Prov. 15:33). The balanced nature of Jesus' teaching on humility is shown in His statement that the greatest commandment concerning human interpersonal relationships is, "You shall love your neighbor as yourself" (Matt. 22:39). Here is no call for debasement of self, but a recognition that a man who does not like himself can never adequately love anyone else. Each individual—four or forty years old—is a person of worth in the sight of God. Each is one for whom God sent His Son.

The apostle Paul reemphasizes this concept of self-worth in his teachings on marriage: "So husbands ought also to love their own wives as their own bodies. He who loves his own wife loves himself; for no one ever hated his own flesh, but nourishes and cherishes it, just as Christ also does the church" (Eph. 5:28,29). The Bible clearly recognizes the importance of a healthy, realistic self-concept in human growth and experience.

THE POWER OF THE CHILD'S SELF-IMAGE

Generally, we accept people at face value, for what

they seem to be. We often consider the worth of a person on the basis of his observed behavior. Since most people develop specific patterns of action in certain situations, a classification seems to simplify many interpersonal relationships. So a system based on outward activity is the easiest to apply.

However, a man is likely to avoid judging himself by the same external standard he applies to others, since he recognizes that there are facets of himself that others do not perceive. Thus, adults develop skill at putting on masks, presenting that part of their personality that seems best suited to the situation.

The young child has not become adept at such a ploy. His feelings are close to the surface, and he expresses his attitude by his action. Careful observation of a child's behavior shows how his entire relationship to life is determined by his self-image.

The child who is expected to succeed, who is given encouragement and appropriate guidance, develops the confidence that makes success possible. The child who is surrounded by evidence of his inability and successive failures has a great hurdle to overcome in ever developing feelings of achievement.

Since the young child's thought processes are limited to recognizing only his viewpoint (he expects everyone else to see and feel just as he does), it is obvious that his attitude about himself is a compelling force in determining the quality of his behavior. If he feels happy to be who he is and enjoys the wonders of childhood, it is inconceivable to him that he could possibly feel any other way about himself. But if the child feels himself as unworthy and unlovable, no other option seems accessible to him.

Add to his limited frame of reference, the seeming omniscience and omnipotence of the adults in his life. He views them as truly marvelous beings with amazing powers. So he has no reason in his early years to question anything they say or do. If they reflect to him a feeling that he is wanted, and is an important part of their life, how could he question his value to them? But if they make him feel like a nuisance, always in the way, he will accept their verdict as being accurate. The child's concept of himself is a mirror image of how he sees himself reflected in the behavior of other people.

The child who constantly hears that he is "bad," "naughty," "a lot of trouble," or "never gonna amount to nothin' " will accept these judgments as being accurate portrayals of who he is, and will most likely live up to the picture. And from that vantage point, he will view his world and its Creator as hostile to his desires. Parents and teachers concerned with guiding a child into the Christian faith need to carefully consider the powerful significance of the child's self-image.

WHAT IS A POSITIVE SELF-IMAGE

A person, child or adult, forms his self-image from a host of impressions, experiences and encounters. However, there are several major ingredients which contribute to a child's positive self-concept.

The security of belonging

A sense of belonging is basic to acquiring a sense of worth. The feelings of love and safety that parents communicate to the infant in the way they hold him, care for him, and play with him help to establish a basic sense of trust. The child needs to feel that his place in the family is unconditional. He is accepted wholeheartedly just as he is, and need not fear rejection or abandonment if his performance falls short of parental expectations. Acceptance by individuals and groups beyond the family circle strengthen his growing confidence. As his needs are met willingly, he feels that he belongs.

The satisfaction of achievement

A child experiences enormous satisfaction from his rapidly expanding capabilities. Most of the objects in his world are beyond his ability to master, so toys are introduced that he can adequately handle. Observant parents provide him with a variety of appropriate things to look at, touch, chew, shake and pound. Each new activity usually produces the deep satisfaction of successful mastery. When the three-year-old defiantly announces, "I'd rather do it myself!" he is demonstrating his deep need for accomplishment. Control over his body and the development of skills that make him increasingly self-sufficient, are fuel for self-confidence. The old adage holds true in early childhood just as in the business world: Nothing succeeds like success.

The joy of feeling valued

The first two ingredients of positive self-image (belonging and achievement) combine to form a powerful third force. When the child succeeds at an activity and the people to whom he looks for his sense of belonging show that the action was important, the child is well on his way to feeling he is worthwhile. The recognition he receives with each new feat meets a deep human need to feel that he has significance to those about him. The assurance that he is valued is transmitted to the child through human channels. These messages of praise and recognition form a necessary foundation for receiving the ultimate message of Good News. The love of parents and teachers, demonstrated in countless small and subtle ways, prepares the child for the overwhelming thought that God loves him. While theologians through the ages have stumbled at the idea of almighty God taking any interest in the menial affairs of men, a young child who has been nurtured by loving adults finds the fact that God loves and cares for him very easy to accept. "My parents love and value me. So why shouldn't God?" he reasons.

What can possibly lift the soul of man or child higher than the powerful impact of knowing God is deeply and lovingly concerned about his life? This great truth forms the cornerstone of the Christian's self-image.

THE PARENTS' SELF-IMAGE

The most important thing adults can do to help build a healthy self-image in a child is to possess a positive self-image of their own. Far too many scars are transmitted to children as parents express their own deep-seated frustrations, ambitions and resentments.

Must parents then be free of problems in order to raise healthy children? Of course not! However, parents need to learn how to cope with the difficulties acceptably. The child should never be used as a means by which adults work out their problems.

How often has a child become the battle prize in a struggle between husband and wife, each seeking to bolster his pride by winning the child's affection and support as an ally in the conflict! How many parents who feel they were deprived of an opportunity as a child determine to give exactly that opportunity to their son or daughter, not recognizing that each person is unique. The child may not have the same interest or need that is driving Mom or Dad. Parental efforts to regain lost opportunities through a child can be damaging to that child's self-esteem. He begins to question whether he has any real personal identity, or if he is just an extension of his parent's ambitions.

Parental stability is extremely crucial since the parent-child relationship is a highly dynamic one. Parents do not merely relate to passively receptive children. Parents must continually react to the behavior of each child as an individual. And each child, even before birth, is a uniquely behaving personality. Within the same family, one baby can be so "good," sleeping through the night, quietly playing in its crib, and the next one be very "fussy" or "colicky" and keep both parents going all the time. It is important for parents to recognize that these physical, temperamental differences can be reinforced by parental responses.

The quiet baby may be frequently cuddled and played with, while the active one is wrestled and argued with. The placid one senses real pleasure in relationships with people, while the aggressive baby feels surrounded by tension. Both will react accordingly. The response of parents, teachers and other adults is likely to continue on the same basis. Ultimately, this chain of responses can lead to some deep-seated attitudinal differences within parents toward the children. Consequently the unhappy child may begin to see himself as unlovable.

In the same way, parents with unresolved emotional problems can transmit their fears and frustrations to their children very early in life. "The quality of feeding and handling associated with mothering helps the infant to develop a sense of trust in the earliest months of life. . . . It is on this important foundation of trust that a person's orientation toward others and toward his environment is to be built."[3]

The man or woman who lacks a sense of personal value and worth will have little to offer the growing child's self-image. The person who does not really like himself will find it extremely difficult to help a child develop wholesome feelings about himself. A basic principle of child nurture is, "You nourish from overflow, not from emptiness."[4] For the sake of a strong, long-lasting relationship, parents and teachers must learn to meet their emotional needs by their own efforts, and not depend on children to fill a void.

At this specific point many people find their Christian faith especially meaningful. A vital, confident relationship with the Lord Jesus Christ gives people a new perspective of their own worth as human beings. To the Christian, there is no concept more conducive to a positive feeling about self than the belief that God cares personally for each individual. The Christian who has learned to live in that assurance has taken a first step in becoming the kind of person that can nourish from strength.

A rigorous self-examination often helps parents and teachers to pinpoint areas of their life that may need attention. "How do I really feel about myself?" "How do I really feel about my children?" "What are my true ambitions for my children?" "Why have I selected these?" "How are the children responding to these goals?" "Are these realistic goals that allow each child to be unique?" Such questions can get the process in gear. Husbands and wives need to talk over these questions together. Parents and teachers should wrestle these issues with each other. A qualified third party should be consulted if serious problems or disagreements seem to surface.

A human being's attitudes and feelings are not set in concrete, but retain amazing potential for adjustment and adaptation. However, during the years of early childhood, basic attitudes toward life and the all-important feeling about self are established. Only with diligent effort can they be altered later on. Parents and teachers owe it to themselves to exert that effort to build their own self-esteem. But they also owe it to their children to be able to nourish from strength. An excellent help for parents and teachers in examining their own self-image is Lloyd Ahlem's book, *Do I Have to Be Me?* (Regal Books, 1973).

PRINCIPLES FOR BUILDING SELF-IMAGE

The adult who has come to grips with the development of his own self-image needs to begin establishing appropriate guidelines to help a child acquire a positive self-concept. An obviously tired young mother was waiting in line at an airport while her twin five-year-old boys made themselves obnoxious by running and screaming through the concourse. Aware that her boys were attracting a great deal of unfavorable comment from fellow passengers, the mother would occasionally proffer a weak, "Settle down now, boys," with absolutely no effect on their raucous behavior. The boys were very much aware that, at that moment at least, what mother said and what mother intended to enforce were two different things. And the look in the mother's eyes showed that she knew well she faced a long flight with two small tyrants whom she was unable to control. Parenthood under these conditions is not only unenjoyable, it is a wearisome duty that erodes the self-esteem of the parent and robs the child of needed security.

Establish and enforce reasonable rules

Rules and standards that are reasonable and that are consistently enforced help parents maintain their own sense of identity and give children a stable framework for building a worthwhile self-image.

Too many restrictions, however, can be just as damaging to the parent-child relationship, and thus to the child's growing self-image, as too few. Rules should be established for the benefit of both adults and children, and should be appropriate to the child's stage of development. Wise parents realize that a one-year-old needs to explore and experiment. They meet this need by arranging his surroundings to allow exploration with safety.

The two-year-old experimenting with language to communicate his wishes and feelings is apt to automatically answer no to almost any request. Parents should recognize that this behavior is not incipient rebellion that needs to be nipped in the bud with harsh punishment. It is rather the little tyke's attempt to learn what it means to be an individual. Parental guidance needs to be firm, but always suited to the child's ability to understand and respond. Telling a child that a rule must be obeyed "because I say so," is really an admission that it is not a very good rule. Paul instructed parents to avoid exasperating and discouraging children (Col. 3:21), which are the results of inappropriate and inconsistent rules. Acceptable behavior will only be forthcoming when the rule and the reason for it have been communicated to a child in terms he can understand.

Give specific instruction

Mrs. Lasher was continually distraught at the constant state of upheaval in her three-year-old's room. Her repeated commands to Margie to "clean up and put away your toys," produced results far short of Mother's wishes. Finally, she realized that Margie simply did not understand what was expected of her. The instructions were too general. When Mrs. Lasher took the time to work with Margie and give her specific directions, one at a time, the job was completed. Best of all, both Margie and Mother felt much better about the entire situation. A source of much irritation was removed from the relationship.

Accept honest emotions

Parents need to make rules in a climate of honest acceptance. Many times a young child may understand the reason for a decision, but he still does not like it. These feelings are his emotional reaction to having his desire thwarted, or having something disliked imposed upon him. A child's emotions are not always under his voluntary control. Unhappiness, fear, anger, frustration do not evaporate just because Mom or Dad gives an order that they should.

Even parents who recognize how moods and emotions affect their own behavior often treat children as though feelings could be turned on or off at will. Every adult knows that just saying, "Cheer up," can never chase a mood of depression. No amount of verbal cajoling by well-wishers can make unhappiness disappear. Yet, parents persist in struggling with a child, telling him he is silly, stubborn, perverse, disobedient, childish and a host of other adjectives in an attempt to persuade him to disown an emotional state that to him is very real.

Who would be so unthinking as to tell a bereaved widow not to feel lonely because she will "get over it" eventually? Such comments would only add to the widow's emotional burden. Truly sympathetic friends look for ways to express their understanding and empathy for her feelings of loss.

Children, however, are often refused similar respect as they try to handle a strong emotion, especially if it is considered to be improper. It is at these times that the child's feelings need to be accepted. And he needs an adult's help in learning to handle these feelings.

Don was very upset and intent on revenge when Ricky accidentally knocked down his pile of blocks. His teacher alertly intercepted Donny, recognizing his desire to commit mayhem. "Don, I know you must be angry that Ricky knocked down your pile of blocks. I watched how hard you worked to build it up. I know you feel very mad that your work was spoiled." She understood his anger without condemning him for it. But she also made it very clear that she could not allow him to harm Ricky. As Don's hostility began to diminish, she redirected his attention to another activity. The crisis passed. Had the teacher told Don to stop being angry, he would have been unable to comply. He would have felt both he and his feelings had been rejected.

There is no substitute for honesty in a healthy parent-child relationship. A child will only feel safely accepted by the adults in his life when he knows he can be himself and will still be loved. This climate eliminates the corrosive problems of deceit and subterfuge that underlie the communications breakdown of the generation gap.

Provide for healthy activity

In addition to establishing suitable rules that are consistently enforced, parents and teachers contribute to a child's self-image by providing a variety of activity appropriate to the child's age level. As one veteran teacher once said, "There is no such thing as a bored two-year-old." If something is not provided for them to do, they will find something. Elaborate toys are unnecessary. However, the child should be provided with a variety of safe and interesting objects to manipulate.

One of the key ingredients of a positive self-image is acquiring the ability to achieve. As the young child experiments and works with toys and other materials in his environment he develops certain skills. Learning to dress himself and tie his shoes give a child great satisfaction in accomplishment. "I wanna help," is a common plea, which many parents believe is usually uttered either when the family is in a hurry or when the task is very difficult.

However, while it is true that the young child's "help" is usually more of a hindrance than an assist, the patient and understanding parent will be frequently rewarded with the priceless beam of happiness on the face of a proud boy or girl. "Look! I did it myself!"

Offer praise for accomplishment

Closely tied to feelings of success is the reinforcement that comes with parental praise. Positive recognition from Mom and Dad has a powerful effect on the behavior and attitude of a young child, far more powerful than punishment for failure. Positive reinforcement for desirable behavior satisfies the child's need for attention, strengthens the likelihood that the action will be repeated and builds his feelings of achievement.

However, evaluations of a child's performance should be realistic. To proclaim every action as a great accomplishment can only lead to cheapening the recognition. Eric grew tired of having every picture he drew declared to be "a simply beautiful picture." He finally asked, "What do I have to do to draw a bad one?"

Praise should be directed at the child's performance, not at his person. Both negative and positive evaluations can be very threatening to a child if he sees them as statements of the kind of person he is. Labels put unnecessary and often harmful pressure on the child. Rather than calling a child "a bad boy," it is better to specify that the action was unacceptable. "Leaving your tricycle on the sidewalk is dangerous; someone might fall over it," identifies the undesirable behavior. Criticism can be a subtle problem when it brings a child to perceive his personal status is dependent on his performance.

Kirsten's father had followed a pattern of rewarding her for acceptable behavior by lavishing her with love and telling her what a good girl she was. Very real feelings of insecurity began to appear in Kirsten as she came to believe that she was loved only when she excelled. This demand for performance caused her stress and worry. It limited her concept of self-worth. These problems could have been avoided had her father made clear to her that she was always acceptable, regardless of her abilities. Parents can express reactions by statements such as, "I like the way you put away your blocks," "Thank you," "Your picking up the papers was a big help to me." Avoid attaching value judgments to the child by the use of phrases such as, "You're such a good boy" or "You're so nice to do that."

Give a child focused attention

Interacting purposefully with a child at a meaningful level requires that parents be sensitively alert to their child as a unique individual. This involves displaying a quality of respect for the child as a family member and human being with rights and privileges. It does not signify that the parent should abdicate his own rights, for parents are also humans. Dorothy Briggs refers to this attitude as one of "focused attention" in which the parent establishes times to become involved with the child at a personal level.[5] Roger's father made it a point to spend some time alone with his son every day. Frequently, however, the father's mind was somewhere else. As this quality of inattentiveness became a pattern, the father-son times became less and less meaningful to both of them. Roger grew up sharing few interests and having little significant communication with his father.

Sherri's father planned his day so he could give her his full attention for at least a brief period. He found many things he considered ordinary took on a new dimension of interest when he began sharing them with his daughter. Watching a caterpillar inch its way up a tree, he asked her, "How many legs does it have?"

"It keeps moving them. I can't count them," Sherri answered.

"Does he move them all at the same time?" he asked. As their examination of the insect continued, he found that, far from being a chore, this interaction with Sherri was delightful. Each day new experiences brought new discoveries and enjoyments. Sherri gave her sense of wonder to each encounter and Dad contributed his knowledge and vocabulary. Dad treated her as a person worthy of being the center of his interest at these times. This kind of focused attention helped Sherri build a healthy view of herself and a lasting relationship with her father.

ACTIVITIES FOR BUILDING A POSITIVE SELF-IMAGE

Conversation

Helping the young child develop language skills to understand others and to communicate his thought is a major factor in helping him to build a positive self-image. In homes of low achievement children, it has been repeatedly observed that verbal communication is at a bare minimum.[6] This lack has a definitely negative effect on the child's self-esteem. A child needs to hear his own name often in a positive context. The child's name is more than just a label that he wears. It embodies for him the very essence of his total personality. Three-year-old Karen demonstrated this feeling when her father teasingly asked her if her fondness for cookies meant she was a cookie monster. "I'm not a cookie monster!" she declared. "I'm a Karen!" She saw herself as not just a little girl who happened to be referred to as Karen. Karen was what she was. Frequent use of the child's name helps him to develop his self-identity. Use of his name in positive settings helps him to feel good about that identity. "I've always hated my middle name," confessed a successful businessman. "I think I feel that way because when I was a child, my mother only used it when she was mad at me."

As children engage in activity, they often tend to produce a steady stream of words describing their behavior. This is not intended to communicate to anyone, but is evidently very important to their developing thought processes. Adults can assist by talking with the child about the details of whatever is transpiring. Ask simple questions to help a child discover interesting features of an object or situation.

"There goes a train. Can you make a noise like a train? . . . Is that train larger or smaller than our car?"

"You're having a good time, aren't you? It's fun to climb those bars."

"I'm making sandwiches for lunch today. First we get out the bread. Now what do we need? Where do we keep the mayonnaise?"

"Before we eat I want to thank God for our food. I am

so glad we can all be together, I want to thank God for that, too."

"You have such strong arms to lift those big blocks. Who made your strong arms? . . . God made your strong arms."

Children respond positively to this kind of attention. Words that identify actions and objections help a child become increasingly aware of his surroundings. When a child calls an adult's attention to a seemingly commonplace object or event, ask simple questions (appropriate to his age level) to help the child extend his knowledge and/or clarify his thoughts. "How do you feel about it? What do you like about it? What would you like to do with it?" Help the child to focus his attention on aspects of his surroundings. Just as important, perhaps, are the manifold insights that adults receive into how children think when the doors of communication are kept open.

Karen's mother was startled to find her five-year-old going through a new Bible storybook and circling the word "God" wherever it appeared on the page. Stifling her first reaction to reprimand the child for defacing a book, she quietly asked, "Why are you doing that?"

Karen's matter-of-fact answer was, "So that I will know where to find God when I want Him."

One particular type of conversation to be avoided is discussion of the child in his presence. Jimmy's grandmother brought him to Sunday School for the first time and felt it necessary to tell the teacher, "Jimmy's parents were divorced about six months ago and he hardly ever sees his father. He has become a real problem because of that." The grandmother and the teacher were talking to each other, but anyone looking at Jimmy could not miss seeing the hurt look that came on his face as he heard the conversation.

Unthinking adults often discuss the most intimate details of a child's life in a way they would find ill-mannered if they were speaking about an adult. After having this called to her attention one mother admitted, "I would be dreadfully humiliated if I heard my husband discussing my problems. Yet I never dreamed of giving my children the same courtesy I expected."

Besides causing embarrassment, discussing a child in his presence is treating him as if he were not there. Few actions can be more damaging to any person's self-image.

Music

Singing is another important avenue of communication. Even the most unmusical parents can open an enjoyable vista of expression to a child by singing frequently in his presence. Take the time to learn a few simple children's songs, both humorous and serious, secular and Christian.

Make up words to fit simple tunes. Sing about your child's everyday experiences. For instance, to "Farmer in the Dell" tune, sing:

(Tom) is glad today.
Yes, (Tom) is glad today.
He's glad because he has new shoes,
Yes, (Tom) is glad today.

Vary the third line to fit the occasion. Or, sing, "He's glad because the Lord loves him. . . ."

Growth patterns

As the child grows, the changes in his size, strength and coordination are as exciting to him as to his parents. Share his enthusiasm by using a growth chart, supplemented with photographs taken at various stages of growth. A family photo album that shows how he and others he knows are changing also helps him see how he is "growing taller and stronger, just as God planned."

Select a plant or a tree for you and your child to observe its growth and seasonal changes. Relate these transformations to the child's development. "See how pretty and green our tree is. Do you remember when it was bare and looked so cold and lonely? God planned for many kinds of trees to get new leaves every year. And God planned for you to keep growing taller and stronger, too."

Cut a piece of string the same length as the child's height. Let him compare the string's length to other objects around the house or classroom. Talk with him about skills he is gaining. Help him to feel your sense of pride in the many things he has learned to do.

Physical skills

Two-year-olds are not quite ready to put on a catcher's mitt and start tossing a few with Dad. But there are many things they can do with balls that are fun, helpful to physical coordination, and that give feelings of satisfaction in bodily control. Also, the activities help the child and the adult to enjoy interacting with each other, a critical ingredient to the self-image of both.

A young child will enjoy a great sense of accomplishment in imitating an adult model by following simple directions in handling a ball. Give one simple instruction at a time. "Hold the ball in both hands. . . . That's right! Now stretch both hands straight out in front. . . . Now put the ball in just one hand. . . . Now put it in the other hand!"

An older child will be able to hold the ball out to his side, over his head, and behind his back. All ages enjoy rolling a ball over their bodies. This activity provides a good opportunity to build awareness of body parts. Holding a ball between the feet or knees and hopping (or walking) is a good test of agility. Encourage children to think of creative things they can do with the ball.

Many materials have become staples of early childhood programs because of their effectiveness in helping the child to improve his physical competency. Puzzles are a challenge to eye-hand coordination and small muscle development. Blocks of varying sizes and shapes help the child develop his manipulative skills, as well as to exercise his ability to plan and carry out an idea. Modeling clay and dough offer opportunities for creating with no fear of failure since mistakes can always be squeezed out and a fresh start made. Finger painting, gadget printing, collages, easel painting and cut-and-paste projects are creative art experiences that allow a child the freedom to create something that is uniquely his own. Asking a child to "Tell me about your picture" opens fascinating horizons for understanding and growth for both the child and the adult.

Independence training

Closely related to the development of physical competence is the cultivation of independence. During the first years of life the child makes dramatic strides from being totally dependent to becoming amazingly competent to care for many of his basic needs. Each step in the development of independence has the potential for adding substantially to the child's positive self-concept.

Unfortunately, adults often needlessly delay the child's assumption of many daily functions. Sometimes adults actively encourage children to be dependent as a way of satisfying the adult's need to be needed. This kind of guidance also damages the child's development.

Parents and teachers should consciously examine everything they do for a child, asking, "How much of this activity could he do by himself?" Giving praise for each accomplishment will help the child enjoy the experience and increase his desire to do it again. It will also insure against the child feeling that self-reliance results in less attention, a very discouraging prospect for all children.

Games

While riding in the car, ask a child to look for a green truck, a yellow house, or an alphabet letter on a sign. Invite him to join you in this game. Ask him what his hands can do that his nose cannot, or what he can do with his ears that he cannot do with his elbows. This game can be played verbally or can be pantomimed.

Mothers have been playing games with babies from the beginning of time. These kinds of simple games are valuable in helping the child develop abilities to perceive and move. "This little pig went to market, . . ." is a longtime favorite because it is fun. It is an example of many games that produce growing awareness of parts of the body.

Peekaboo is a favorite of little ones. The game can be varied infinitely with different objects and hiding places. Hide-and-seek for twos and threes is only slightly removed from infant peekaboo. The fun of the game for the child is finding, not hiding or seeking. Children will "hide" in very obvious places, call out to tell you where they are, and laugh uproariously when they are found. They see nothing incongruous about reusing the same hiding place repeatedly, and are likely to become upset if they are unable to find their partner quickly.

Many fours and fives continue the same pattern and only gradually begin to see it as a game where the object is to remain hidden until found.

Participation is the main objective for a young child in a game. Winning is a very fuzzy concept. Games for young children should be those in which "Everybody won!" Older fives begin to understand that in competition a winner produces a loser. Competitive games are not appropriate for building self-image in early childhood. Instead, use games that stress cooperation and participation.

In all activities, the adult should seek to give the child enjoyable, successful experiences that develop feelings of value. The early experiences of life are highly crucial to a child's concept of himself. " 'As the twig is bent . . .' has long been part of Western folklore. Scientific data supports this view. The origins of self lie in the early years. How the child will see himself is influenced by the way he is treated, the opportunities provided for him, how he is evaluated as he copes with these opportunities, and how he perceives these evaluations."[7]

Notes

1. Munsinger, *Fundamentals of Child Development,* p. 403.
2. Briggs, *Your Child's Self-Esteem,* p. 3.
3. Bruce Grossman, "Enhancing the Self," in *Exceptional Children,* 1971, vol. 38, pp. 249-254.
4. Briggs, *Your Child's Self-Esteem,* p. 55.
5. Ibid., p. 64 ff.
6. Munsinger, *Fundamentals of Child Development,* p. 384.
7. Ira Gordon, "The Beginnings of the Self," in Anderson, Robert and Shane, Harold (Eds.) *As the Twig Is Bent* (Boston: Houghton Mifflin, 1971), p. 142.

CHAPTER THREE

The Child and Others

"Tommy, this is Peter, and he would like to play with you. Would you share one of your trucks with him?"

(Two-year-old Tommy remains silent, and pulls both trucks closer to himself.)

"If you both had a truck, you could have fun playing together."

(More silence. Tighter grip on the trucks.)

"Which truck would you like Peter to play with, the red one or the blue one?"

(Tommy clutches both trucks to his chest.)

"Here, Peter, you can play with these blocks until Tommy is through playing with the trucks."

Sharing and cooperation are not within the understanding of a young child. Even though adults cajole and entice, he tends to be suspicious of requests to part with the toy he is using.

Sensing that this possessive attitude signals the beginning of a lifetime of selfishness, concerned adults often become overzealous in their efforts to teach the child to take turns and share. The resulting howls of displeasure can be heard repeatedly from little mouths whose owners vigorously resist these socialization efforts. Much of the strain and unhappiness of this process could be diminished if parents and teachers realized how the child views these encounters.

The infant begins life unable to distinguish between himself and his surroundings. What a gigantic learning task lies just ahead! During his early months he refines his perceptions, but remains unable to recognize that objects exist outside of his immediate awareness. He will follow an object with his eyes, or reach clumsily for it with his arms, but if it passes from his line of vision he will act as though it has ceased to exist. After he is about six months old, he will begin to look for the object that disappeared, but will only repeat whatever action he was performing at the moment of disappearance. By ten months, he may begin to actively search for the object, but will look only in places where it has been found before. Jean Piaget, the noted Swiss psychologist, has indicated that it is not until the latter part of the second year of life that a child is able to think about an object that is not physically present. Piaget stresses that it takes nearly two years of exposure and interaction with things and people before the child is capable of realizing they exist permanently and are independent of his own actions.[1]

Much of the young child's difficulty in seeing his world objectively stems from his inability to recognize the essential factors in any situation. His attention is drawn to one aspect only and he is unable to deal with two dimensions of a problem simultaneously. This limitation on childlike thought manifests itself repeatedly in the child's experience, often until age six or seven. Most of the young child's illogical actions have their roots in this restricted point of view. He has not encountered enough of the world to be able to think about a specific fact and come to a general conclusion. Nor can he take a general principle and apply it to a specific action. Rather, he is limited to using a particular fact to lead him to another particular fact. Since he selects those aspects of a situation that seem most interesting to him at the moment, and does not possess an organizing principle, he often relates things to each other in a very unique and inappropriate manner.[2] Such was the case when the three-year-old boldly announced, "I haven't had my bath, so it isn't nighttime!" These two common events had always occurred together in his experience. So he reasoned that one depended on the other. He was unable to see the larger circumstance.

THE CHILD AND THINGS

The young child's view of the world centers on himself. All the action of the things in his environment seems to revolve around him and his desires. Very gradually he comes to see that these things have an existence of their own and are not dependent on him for their actions. He also perceives that events seem to depend on adults who appear all-powerful. Things are pushed and pulled, opened and closed, all for the child's benefit and all by masterful adults.[3]

A child gives thoughts and feelings to many of the objects in his world. Dolls and teddy bears talk and make decisions. Quite often the child attributes his own emotions or desires to these inanimate objects. This aspect of a child's thought process was shown very dramatically following the 1971 earthquake in Southern California when many young children refused to get in their beds the evening following the quake. They were convinced that all of the upset had been caused by their cribs in which they were asleep at the moment the earthquake hit. Their fears were directed squarely at the offending beds.

Piaget noted in his observations of young children that this kind of outlook gradually diminishes and has largely disappeared by age six or seven. Those objects that remain stationary lose their reputation for being alive sooner than things that move or grow, such as cars or plants.[4]

Gradually, as the child ceases to view objects as being alive in the same sense people are alive, he begins to attribute their movement and their very existence to human operations. This viewpoint is the natural outgrowth of seeing adults manipulate the world in so many wonderful ways. Again applying his practice of relating one specific to another, he often sees such phenomena as the sun and moon acting in response to human direction.

Parents and teachers who desire for a child to know that God made the world and everything in it (Acts 17:24) need to consider carefully the way in which they will present this fact. The problem is not one of disbelief, for the young child is very willing to accept explanations given by adults. The difficulty is in terms of what the explanation will mean to the child.

A two-year-old will accept the statement that God made apples with the same level of understanding if told that General Motors makes Buicks or that Mommy makes cakes. In the mind of a child, these products are all equally wonderful creations. And the sources are not nearly as interesting as the product themselves.

However, by the time he is five, questions of origin have become of real interest, and often entail the "how" as well as the "who" or "what." The questions about the process of creation can come fast and furiously. Some children will be satisfied with "God made it." However, this answer may carry magical visions of a super sorcerer. Other children will demand to know how He made it, or may even deny that He did, since their own experience tells them the object in question came from a store.

Teachers and parents have found it more effective to say that "God planned for apples to grow," rather than leaving a young mind to wrestle with how God went about forming each individual apple. However, any verbal explanation of natural wonders usually gives a child only a superficial understanding at best. Words are still his least effective way to learn.

The most effective way for a child to learn is through firsthand experiences. He needs many encounters with growing things to begin to understand their origins. Through the fun of planting seeds, watering the soil and watching the new growth, he starts to grasp the wonders of life. After repeated firsthand experiences with plant and animal life cycles a child begins to comprehend God as creator. Of course, adults need to interpret these observations and activities in terms of Bible truth. "Do you see any new leaves on our plant today? . . . You found a big one! Let's count the points on it. . . . Only God can make plants grow. *God is good* (Ps. 73:1) to make plants for us to enjoy." The sense of awe that comes from these experiences builds preliminary foundations for a realistic concept of God.

ACTIVITIES FOR LEARNING ABOUT THINGS

What the child learns about the world around him happens spontaneously as he interacts with the materials in his environment. Thus, the adults in his life can play a major role by the decisions they make concerning just what these things will be. From infancy on, the child should be provided with a variety of toys that are safe, interesting and easy to manipulate. Early enjoyment of touching, squeezing and chewing encourages curiosity and self-confidence, essential ingredients for later explorations. Toys must not be too complex as to be frustrating for the young explorer.

Puzzles offer many interesting ways to learn about shapes, color and relationships of objects. While very young children need simple puzzles of three or four large pieces, five-year-olds are often capable of completing puzzles with more than twenty-five pieces. The sense of satisfaction the child receives from problem-solving is a benefit of puzzles. However, working puzzles also sharpens a child's perception of pictures, colors and objects.

A variety of sensory experiences helps children to appreciate the diversity of their world. Recognition games in which the child is limited to the use of one sense are great fun. For example, trying to guess an object just by its sound promotes awareness of the environment. "I'm glad God planned your ears so you can hear that bell ringing." Help a child associate pleasant experiences with God's goodness. Similar games can be played, using only touch or smell for identification. The use of touch is an important part of art experiences, usually considered a visual medium. Working with clay or dough provides an interesting sensory experience. Finger painting is one of the most exciting and enjoyable experiences a child can have! An entirely new dimension can be achieved by adding whipped soap flakes to the paint, then letting the child experiment. As he is enjoying the experience, say, "Thank you God, for Dina's fingers that can make such interesting pictures!" Collages, using materials of differing textures, have great sensory appeal for children. Fabrics, wood, leaves, cereals, sea shells, nut shells, beans and peas and flower petals are just a few of the items that children enjoy touching and arranging, then gluing on a surface. Many of the same objects can be used for rubbings. Place objects on a flat surface, then cover with paper. Then the child rubs a crayon over the paper until the pattern of the objects underneath shows through. The child will grow to appreciate God and His world as you comment, "I like the different kinds of things God made for us. Some things are soft, like this feather. Some things are hard, like these seeds. God made all these things for us to enjoy. God loves us."

Experiences with living things are also significant to the child's learning process. Insects, fish, birds, or other pets provide daily lessons in natural processes, as well as helping him learn respect for living things. Plant growth is often of special interest to a young child because changes usually occur more rapidly than in animals. A bean placed on a wet sponge lets a child observe the growth of both leaves and roots. A sweet potato partly submerged in water offers the same lessons on a larger scale. Seeds planted in the garden or in an indoor planter often show fascinating changes within just a few weeks. Provide a good quality magnifying glass to make observation a vastly enriching experience. Simple explanations of what the child can actually observe add to the child's appreciation and understanding, especially when the information comes in answer to the child's questions. "God planned for that little seed to be able to use water so that it can grow and become a big plant. God is so great!"

While sharing the sweet taste of a ripe apple with two-year-olds, Mr. Fitzgerald paused, and said quietly, "Thank you, God, for making good apples for us to eat." The children understood little or nothing of where the apples came from. But they sensed their teacher's reverent attitude of thankfulness to God, a meaningful foundation for future learning.

THE CHILD AND PEOPLE

The newborn infant does not immediately distinguish between things and people. Gradually, however, he becomes aware that people are different. Very soon they become the most interesting part of his world. The way in which they treat him forms the basis for his feelings about himself, and thus about everything else, including God.

Christians have long been grateful to the Lord Jesus for His practice of addressing God as "Father," for this title has given finite minds a means of attempting to grasp the infinite.

The young child's growing concept of God is very powerfully influenced by his relationship with his own parents. Studies have consistently shown that a child's feelings toward his parents have a strong influence on his feelings about God.[5]

The child's behavior is also significantly influenced by the actions of his parents. Parents serve as the primary models for all the child's behavior from infancy on. Often a child will express a desire to "be like Daddy." However, most of a child's imitation of parents occurs unconsciously.

Adult encouragement during a child's performance of a task, and praise when it is completed, exerts a powerful influence on the child's behavior. How very strongly motivated children are to please the significant adults in their lives! This desire to please serves as the basis for the development of a conscience in the young child. When he is able to think of his parents even though they are not physically present, he is able to consciously base his behavior on what he feels will please them. Parental encouragement for acceptable behavior thus lays the foundation for the child's own convictions of what is right.[6]

Observers of young children are often confused by the seeming lack of a relationship between what a child says is right or wrong and the way in which he actually behaves.[7] Much of what the child can express seems to be merely verbalisms with no immediate relationship to his behavior. The reason appears to be tied to the child's inability to give an adequate explanation for actions until he has acquired substantial experience in situations calling for moral judgments. The moral judgments of the young child are dominated by his limited view of the world.[8] The example set by parents and teachers provides a very powerful model for the young child, but he will always react according to the way things appear from his limited viewpoint.

When a child is faced with rules created by all-knowing adults, it does not occur to him to question. Five-year-old Karen announced after her first week at kindergarten that "Robert was a bad boy. He didn't take turns on the swing today." When asked why Robert's actions were wrong, her answer was very firm: "Because Mrs. Meyers said we had to take turns on the swings!" To Karen the rule existed simply because her teacher said so. No thought was given to the common sense of cooperation as the reason behind the rule. The rule was sacred and no questions need be asked.

Both Jean Piaget and Lawrence Kohlberg have identified six major aspects of the young child's moral judgments, which distinguish his thinking from more mature children and adults. Both investigators see these factors as developing independently so that a child may be advanced in one category and immature in another. They found most of these factors present in almost all children until seven or eight years of age. They recognize, however, that both intelligence and specific experiences could alter the rate of growth in either direction.

First, the young child judges an act as right or wrong on the physical consequences, not on the motives of the individual involved. Spilling milk is no less an offense to the child if unintentional than if done on purpose. Accidental damage is just as culpable as intentional mayhem. The child does temper the judgments of his own misdeeds sooner than he does for someone else.

Second, a young child judges actions as either right or wrong with no middle ground. He expects everyone else to share this evaluation.

Third, his judgment is strongly influenced by the reactions of others. If the action is punished, it is bad; if rewarded, it is good. This practice stems from the child's total acceptance of adults as sources of rules and rewards. Evidence shows, however, that this evaluation does break down if responses are vastly out of line with the reaction the child has come to expect.

Fourth, the young child does not think of the cooperative benefits in his behavior towards others. He does not seek to elicit kindness by being kind. He is only interested in how the other person will behave toward him. He does not see his own behavior toward others as significant in influencing their actions.

Fifth, young children view punishment as a necessary balance for the wrongdoing. However, they give no thought to actual restitution. A spanking or similar punishment seems to elicit a sense of relief, for it removes the feelings of guilt. The child rarely thinks of some type of effort to undo the damage. He is not usually interested in the idea if it is suggested.

The sixth aspect of immature moral judgment is a tendency to view misfortune as the natural outcome of some misbehavior. Three- and four-year-olds often view inanimate objects as transmitters of deserved punishment.

Thus a child sees falling down as the expected outcome of disobedience. The ground conspires to make it happen. Much of this thinking may be the result of such parental admonitions as, "Don't come crying to me, I warned you not to do that; you just got what you deserved."[9,10]

Because of the limitations of childish thought, attempts that require a child to express verbally adult moral views have proven to succeed at only a very superficial level. Adults concerned about developing Christian ethics in the young child would do far better to focus their attention on the type of models they are providing for childish imitation. Since action precedes language with the young child, strictly verbal attempts to guide moral growth are generally ineffective for this age level.

ACTIVITIES FOR LEARNING ABOUT PEOPLE

Learning about adults

Nothing helps a child learn how to relate to people more effectively than providing him with meaningful interaction with understanding and loving adults. The Bible consistently identifies parents as the adults with this responsibility. The child loves others only as he has been loved. He respects the rights of family members in accord with the respect he has received. He seeks to share and help as he has been helped. Parents who claim they have given a child everything he needs, often omit the most essential factor for helping him learn how to live a purposeful life—themselves.

Many parents unknowingly yet skillfully teach their children negative ways of behaving through consistent patterns of psychological neglect. Maria's situation is sadly typical. Her mother ignored Maria's attempts to get her attention. Maria kept trying to gain a response. Each attempt was louder than the last. By the time her mother did respond, both were irritated. Communication that could have been enjoyable for both became an ordeal. As this pattern was consistently repeated, Maria developed negative feelings about herself and her mother, all because her mother did not understand her child's need to be loved and valued.

Teachers must recognize a child's deep longing to be valued. They need to provide personal attention for each child. As the child builds a personal relationship with the teacher he begins to accept the teacher as a model for his behavior.

In addition to parents and teachers, children need contact with many other adults. It is important to assist the child in viewing neighbors, postmen, store clerks, librarians and others as friendly helpers. Within the Christian community, pastors, missionaries and other church workers can help in the child's growing understandings of adults, to the degree the child is allowed personal contact with them.

Learning about peers

Associations with other children of similar ages are essential for developing a child's interpersonal relationships. While young children are intensely interested in other young children, they do not always find it easy to develop friendships. Often, other children are seen as potential threats to a child's domain.

Jesus very clearly made loving behavior towards

others a cornerstone of the Christian faith. "Love your neighbor as . . . yourself" (Matt. 22:39, *TLB*) is the second greatest of all God's commandments. "If you have love for one another" (John 13:35), Jesus told His disciples, then "men will know that you are My disciples."

The child becomes capable of loving as he has first received love and as he learns to interact with other people. Love is never experienced in the abstract or at long distance. It is always a personal, intimate experience. The growing child needs a foundation of positive interactions with other children as a basis for loving expressions. A Sunday School that talks and sings about loving one another and being kind friends, but provides no opportunity for children to talk to each other, is a classic case of contradictions.

As the child experiences the ups and downs, the give and take of playing with others, he learns some of the most important lessons of his life. Sensitive adults can help the child in this process by providing appropriate equipment, adequate space and just enough supervision to keep everyone safe.

For children who are unable to share a toy, having duplicates of the popular pieces of equipment, such as toy telephones, can ease feelings of uncertainty. Also, many games can help lay a foundation for enjoyable sharing. Variations of "peekaboo," the all-time favorite for one-year-olds, can help a little one feel he can still enjoy a toy, even though it is not in his immediate possession. Hide from view (under a towel) a favorite toy of the child. Wait a moment, then remove the towel with a flourish. The demand for many repetitions of this feat is evidence that the child is learning that surrendering a toy can sometimes be more fun than holding on to it. Rolling a ball back and forth with a two-year-old is another way of developing good feelings about sharing. Including another child in either game adds to the fun. "Charles and Bobby are good friends. I thank God for good friends." Three-year-olds love "hide-and-seek," as long as the hiding places are fairly obvious. The fun is in the finding, not in the seeking. The greatest asset is that hide-and-seek requires at least two to play.

Playing house and building with blocks are absorbing activities for four- and five-year-olds. Conflicts will arise, of course, but the desire for a playmate is strong enough that children generally exert the necessary efforts to overcome problems. The result is a valuable learning experience. Adult reinforcement of desired behavior adds greatly to the likelihood of that behavior reoccurring.

Some children need special help in learning how to play with other children. They have difficulty showing love if they are unable to communicate. Sometimes in busy classrooms or playgrounds where there is a great deal of activity, teachers miss noticing that some children always play alone, even when surrounded by others. While solitary play can be very satisfying to a child at times, it can be highly demoralizing when it results, not from choice, but from lack of ability to relate.

One approach to helping the solitary child is to promote activities that require cooperation. Teeter-totter, sandboxes, block-building, water play, are activities that are more fun for two children than one. Identify the good feelings with words. "David, you and Raymond are really playing well together. You are kind friends. The Bible says, 'Be kind to each other.' " However, some children will rigorously avoid these activities rather than face the specter of failure in personal relationships.

This situation can often be helped by giving the lonely child access to an attractive activity with the hope of drawing other children to interact with him. One teacher offered a child who had difficulty relating to others the opportunity to paint a piece of playground equipment. He responded enthusiastically. As he began to work, the teacher said, "Some other children might come over and say they want to paint, too. What will you tell them?" He had no answer.

She then offered several possible responses he could make from "No!" to "Yes, but you will have to go to the cabinet to get a brush." With each suggestion she helped the child predict how the other child would respond. Then she withdrew and watched as gradually the other children began to approach him. The confidence he felt from being the center of attention helped him to initiate several brief conversations. He also responded to questions asked by other children.

Notice that the teacher not only arranged an activity in which the lonely boy would be the center of attention, she also provided him with specific conversation ideas to help him take advantage of the situation. It is very common for children, as well as adults, to retreat into silence or to resort to unproductive physical efforts, simply because they do not have the words to use.

Do not compare one child with another, nor should adults foster competition among young children. However, children can be helped by learning from what other children do. Often a child will hold back from a new experience until he has observed the behavior of other children. Then he will try it himself. Commending children in the presence of other children is helpful, if rigorous care is taken to be sure that every child receives the praise he needs. Usually it is the least capable child who needs the most recognition, but who often receives the least.

Statements like the following give recognition to children. They also focus the attention of others on the desired behavior, but do not make some children feel less worthy than others.

"Carlos is showing me that he is ready for our story. He is sitting flat on the rug with his hands in his lap. Andrea is ready, too, and so is David."

"I would like to put your finger painting up on the wall with all the others so that everyone can see the many different ways that children made their designs."

"Everyone who is wearing something green may stand up quietly and tiptoe to the door."

"If you know the answer to my question, let me know by putting your hand on your head. Rachel knows. Hillary knows. Daniel has his hand on his head. Marvin, tell me the answer." "Stan did something the Bible talks about. The Bible says 'share what you have,' and Stan gave some of his Play-Doh to Margie."

Children can become more aware of others as individuals in their Sunday School class by hearing the names of other children, as well as their own. For instance, encourage children to draw pictures to send to a specific child who is absent. "Kevin will be very glad to get this picture from his friends. God planned for us to have friends."

One enterprising teacher made up booklets for her kindergartners. On the front of each booklet she lettered the title, "My Friends." Each child was encouraged to ask his friends to do something in the book, such as write their names, draw a picture, outline their hands, or place a thumbprint. The booklet served as a device to encourage children to think about their friends and to interact with other children. The teacher watched for opportunities in which she could call children's attention to God's plan that they love and enjoy their friends. "How glad we are for our friends at church! Thank you, God, for good friends who love us."

Appreciation of individual differences is significant in helping a child acquire a wholesome attitude towards others. Development of perceptual skills through such activities as those mentioned in the section of this chapter on "Activities for Learning About Things" can play a major role in developing a child's awareness of another child's uniqueness. Observing the multitudinous differences in plant and animal life can also help a child enjoy the differences that are part of human experiences. Interaction with children and adults in various settings provides many opportunities to experience these differences. As adults accept and enjoy these differences in age, sex, race, ability, and interest the child will follow this lead. Unfortunately, prejudice and bigotry will also be communicated in the same way. Overriding all other factors, the attitude and behavior of the parents provide a pattern which will either help or hinder the young child in developing a healthy view of God, His world and the people He has made for it.

Notes

1. Jean Piaget, *The Construction of Reality in the Child* (New York: Basic Books, 1954), pp. 76-80.
2. Goldman, *Religious Thinking from Childhood to Adolescence,* p. 95.
3. Piaget, *The Child's Conception of the World,* p. 376.
4. Ibid., pp. 258-259.
5. M. O. Nelson, "The Concept of God and Feelings Toward Parents," in *Journal of Individual Psychology,* 1971, vol. 27, pp. 44-52.
6. P. Brown and R. Elliott, "Control of Aggression in a Nursery School Class," in *Journal of Experimental Child Psychology,* 1965, vol. 2, pp. 103-107.
7. P. H. Whiteman and K. P. Kosier, "Development of Children's Moralistic Judgments," *Child Development,* 1964, vol. 35, pp. 843-850.
8. R. Selman, "Taking Another's Perspective," *Child Development,* 1971, vol. 42, pp. 1721-1734.
9. Jean Piaget, *The Moral Judgment of the Child* (Glencoe, Ill.: Free Press, 1948).
10. Lawrence Kohlberg, "Development of Moral Character and Moral Ideology," in M. Hoffman and L. Hoffman, eds., *Review of Child Development Research,* vol 1 (New York: Russell Sage Foundation, 1964), pp. 396 ff.

CHAPTER FOUR

The Child and the Church

"Is this really God's house?"
"Why do you ask, Jimmy?"
"Well, when I come here He's never home."

Jimmy's question is very natural for a five-year-old, for he understands and uses words in their most literal sense. Derek had a similar reaction when told he was in God's House: "I want to see God's bedroom."

CHURCH FROM A CHILD'S PERSPECTIVE

To the child, the church building is an intriguing and mysterious place. He hears it constantly associated with God. From such phrases as "the house of the Lord," he concludes that the church is the physical dwelling of God. When he also hears that God lives in heaven, confusion results. Although such misunderstandings can usually be explained to the child's satisfaction, it is clear that children under six have a limited understanding of what the church really is.

The child brings the same thought processes to bear on his understanding about the church as he does on any other matter. His viewpoint is dominated by impressions from often irrelevant factors. Young children frequently express the uniqueness of the church in terms of some physical feature of the building, such as a towering spire, colored windows, rows of chairs or big doors. Some children focus on special ceremonies they have witnessed such as weddings, funerals or baptisms as the most important function of the church. Robes, backward collars and big books are often vivid in the child's thinking as essential to the church's operations. These physical features and specific incidents dominate childish thought about what the church is.[1] Four-year-old Jennie protested that an outdoor worship service "really isn't church 'cause I don't have on my white shoes." The young child is likely to fasten his attention on some nonessential factor. Then he convinces himself that is what the church is all about.

WHY WE GO TO CHURCH

The young child has very little insight into the purpose for going to church. Specific actions such as listening to stories, singing songs, holding the Bible, painting pictures and eating crackers are just a few of the motives commonly expressed. "Because it's Sunday," "So Daddy can sleep," and "To make God happy," are some four-year-olds' explanations for church attendance. A child gives these kinds of answers in all seriousness, assured that they explain adequately the real purpose in it all.

Even the child who can give the "right" answer, such as, "To learn about God," "To worship God," or "To study the Bible," usually has no adequate conception of what his words really mean. Further questioning quickly shows his answers are often a mere recitation of statements he has heard from adults.

Underlying many answers is the child's vague feeling that church attendance is some type of trade agreement with God obligating Him to bestow special favors. Or, from the negative side, it is a means for avoiding God's displeasure. Much of the reason for this lack of understanding is that the question simply is not a burning issue for the child. While he may have positive or negative feelings about what happens to him at church, his attendance is not really a decision he must make. The adults in his life decide if he will attend. They notify him of the proper time and take care of transporting him there and back. The child may be happy or unhappy with the decision, but the purpose of it all is not a practical issue to him.

These vague ideas about the reason for attending church also show in the child's awareness of his religious identity. While many five-year-olds may be able to proclaim that they are Baptists, Catholics or Nazarenes, the significance of the label totally escapes them.[2]

WHAT WE DO AT CHURCH

The meaning of specific acts of worship is difficult for a child to grasp. He interprets the things he sees and the words he hears quite literally. Since many of the church sacraments and ceremonies are concealed in symbolism, his understanding at best is very superficial. The symbolism of the Lord's Supper, for example, is beyond the child's understanding, even though he may be able to use the appropriate verbal labels.

"When my mommy gives me a bath she takes my clothes off," was Angie's declaration upon observing her first water baptismal service. The physical properties of this sacrament also tend to dominate the young child's thinking to the exclusion of the symbolic meaning of the act. Exposure to these dramatic portrayals does raise questions for the child. The answers adults give need to be phrased simply, using words the child understands. One thoughtful parent explained, "The Lord Jesus tells us in the Bible to have this special time so we will remember how very much He loves us."

Offerings greatly intrigue a young child. Five-year-old Gordon surprised his parents one Sunday when he announced proudly that Jesus had been in his Sunday School room. Pursuing the matter a little further, they found that the usher who came into the room to pick up the offering container was Gordon's idea of Jesus. Gordon's teachers had carefully explained that the children were giving their money to Jesus. And in Gordon's literal thinking, what could be a more logical conclusion! Gordon and his friends needed a more specific and definite explanation of what happens to offering money.

Also, since young children are not really giving something of their own, but are merely transporting coins given to them for this purpose, giving an offering has only limited value in their learning to share. Attempting to build a habit in a child before he has understood why he is performing in such a way is neither sound educationally nor biblically accurate. Parents and teachers need to explain in simple terms that "we bring our love gift because we love God." Also, showing the child items (Bible, storybooks, materials and equipment) his love-gift money buys helps to clarify this concept for him.

HOW WE BEHAVE AT CHURCH

Children's presence in the church's worship service is often intended by parents as a means to teach their children to sit still in church. This attitude stems partly from the parents' desire for the child not to disturb the parents and other adults during the service. It comes from a conviction that this training is necessary if the child is to behave properly in church services as he grows older. Certain activities are tolerated as cute when the child is three. However, parents fearfully ask, "But what if he acts like that in church when he's thirteen?"

Demanding that a young child sit quietly for an hour or more during a program of no interest to him is a very tall order. Thus some parents resort to threats, bribes or to providing some quiet form of entertainment. Or, hope the child will go to sleep. These measures may succeed in keeping disturbance to a minimum. However, this procedure totally misses the point of introducing the child to worship experiences that are meaningful to him.

Keeping a young child quiet is never difficult when the child finds something that captures his interest. Even one- and two-year-olds will remain involved for extended time periods with an activity in which they are interested. Rather than wrestling with a child to make him sit still in church, parents could more wisely use their energies in helping the church plan a program of interest to the child.

It is better for the young child to spend the church hour in a program designed for his special needs, than to endure an adult meeting where nothing is planned with his capabilities and interest in mind. As the child grows, his attention span will lengthen and his interests will mature. Then an adult worship service will appeal to him, for it will deal with needs he recognizes. However, that time is not during his years of early childhood.

Respect and reverence are also goals that most parents and teachers desire to have children learn by attending an adult church service. Unfortunately, attaining these goals is often reduced to a string of negative commandments for behavior inappropriate in church facilities. The child then sees reverence as a physical thing, rather than an attitude of mind and heart.

One of the problems in helping children to develop reverence is the example set by adults. Not that children see adults running in the halls, yelling over crowds or throwing paper airplanes in the foyer. However, children do see adults in the church building doing all of the normal things they see adults doing elsewhere: standing around, talking with friends, laughing and often drinking coffee. To the child, adult behavior in and near the church buildings does not appear to differ from adult behavior at home, at the store or in the street. Why, then, should children's behavior be expected to differ from the normal activities of children at home or at school? Adults often do an effective job of confusing children with this subtle double standard, using pious declarations as their rationale for banning certain actions for the child.

Children understand far better if unacceptable behavior in a church is explained as disturbing to others or unsafe, rather than as improper. As little Timmy put it when told that God would not like his noise: "Doesn't God like little boys?"

Christians who want children to grow up within the family of the church should make sure the church can accept a child as he is, not as adults wish he were or hope he will become.

HOW WE FEEL ABOUT CHURCH

While the young child's understanding of the church is very limited, and his behavior often seems out of place, he is immensely capable of forming strong feelings about the church and his experiences there. In an interesting survey on this subject, Dr. Ronald Goldman questioned several hundred English children. He discovered that their attitudes toward the church had little to do with their own pattern of attendance. Rather, the single most powerful influence on the child's feelings about church evolved from whether the parents attended church.[3] Parents' interests and attitudes have such strong effect on the child that their feelings actually are dominant over the child's own experience.

Those parents, for whom church attendance is a meaningful part of life, will transmit their feelings to the child, thus preparing him for what then becomes a far more positive experience had their support not existed. When parents show by their words and their manner that they enjoy church participation, the child, seeking to be like them, will imitate their attitude and actions. When parents display negative attitudes concerning church involvement, then this attitude will likely diminish whatever enjoyments the child discovers on his own.

A child's experiences at church, however, cannot be discounted as unimportant. Positive, pleasant experiences make a contribution to a child's concept of church, just as negative encounters can build resistance. The child forms his impressions not from verbal statements about the church, but from the real church that he finds. Both parents and teachers share the responsibility for providing a situation at church that expresses to a child, "Welcome! This place is for you! It has been planned to help you learn of God in the way you learn best—by doing." Participating in activities appropriate to his age-level interests, building stable and meaningful relationships with teachers and children and participating in moments of spontaneous worship, all combine to make a child feel good about his church experience.

If a church could accomplish only one thing with a child through his first five years of life, it should seek to help the child firmly sense that he is loved by the people at church. In this way a foundation is established to help the child see the church as more than a building, but as a group of people who love God and love each other.

ACTIVITIES FOR LEARNING ABOUT CHURCH

The most effective contribution parents can make to a young child's interest in church is to attend regularly themselves. Their example plays a key role in strengthening the child's feelings about church attendance. Conversations with the child concerning his experiences at church can prepare him for what he will discover and will reinforce what he has experienced. Rather than simply asking, "What did you learn at church today?" parents can enrich the child's time at church with such comments as, "Sing one of your Sunday School songs for me," "Let's talk about what you liked best this morning at church" or "Tell me about the story your teacher told you today."

Focusing on a specific part of the child's experience rather than on general topics helps a child recall particular events. When the child brings home a picture he has painted in church school, suggest, "Tell me about your picture." Casual conversations about these things encourage the child to talk about his experiences, often giving an adult opportunity to correct misconceptions. Use the Sunday School curriculum pieces provided by your church to initiate activities that expand on your child's learning at church. A meeting of parents and teachers to discuss such activities as songs, finger fun and creative art can also be helpful.

Since the young child is naturally interested in whatever interests adults, occasional visits to adult worship services can help widen a child's understanding. Church school teachers should consult the pastor for a suitable time for children's visit—preferably during the beginning moments of the service, or, at a time when no service is being held. Perhaps the pastor can meet briefly with the children in the sanctuary.

Before the children visit the sanctuary, help them know where they are going and why; also, a few specific things to look for, such as the large pulpit Bible.

In the sanctuary, direct children's attention to pulpit Bible, offering plates, colorful windows and other unique features of your sanctuary. Sit with the children in the pews for a few minutes to help them sense the beauty and quietness of the sanctuary. Encourage children to carefully examine hymnals. Ask simple questions to help children see colors and designs in windows.

On the way to (or from) the sanctuary, walk by the church sign. Guide children in naming letters in the words shown in the sign. Then let children help you "read" the sign. Also, direct children's attention to your church building cornerstone. Explain briefly what a cornerstone is; read the wording on it. Take a picture of each Bible story class and teacher on the front steps of the church. Also, direct children's attention to the cross or spire atop your church building. Help children know "this cross helps people know this building is a church, a special place to come to learn of God and the Lord Jesus."

You may want to plan two excursions for the children, one to tour the sanctuary and one to examine the things of interest on the outside of your church building. Also, you may want to plan for several small groups of children to tour, one group at a time. When all return to the department room, ask simple questions to help children recall their experience. However, these visits are best when kept brief and treated as special occasions.

A visit to the sanctuary would be most appropriate during a curriculum unit study of the church. However, remember that the part of the church of most importance to a young child is HIS room and the teachers who are with him there.

Several basic things should characterize a program at church designed especially for children. These factors should be consistently present during Sunday School,

Churchtime, Sunday evening or anytime the child is at church. First, the schedule and the content should consider a young child's needs and interests. A child needs involvement with firsthand experiences far more than he needs the secondhand experience of listening to an adult talk. Second, the church is responsible for providing ample space and materials for activities, home-living experiences, block building, observing living plants and animals, puzzles, creative art, children's books and music—ingredients for any good program involving young children.

Music has the unique quality of being able to speak to both the young and old person and should be an important part of a child's experience at church. His enjoyment of a song, for instance, depends upon repeated opportunities to hear and sing it. Seeing pictures and objects that illustrate the words he hears and sings helps to increase his interest and learning. Music in the church school program needs to be carefully selected so as to avoid symbolism and words beyond a child's ability to comprehend. Select songs with words that say exactly what they mean. The words should also express feelings and thoughts with which the young child can easily identify. Singing these songs at home, as well as at church, provides parents with a valuable way to strengthen the bridge between church and home. Learning the songs the child likes to sing at church is an effective way to show what the child does at church is important to parents. And the nice thing about singing with young children is that no matter how off key the adult may be, it doesn't matter to the child! It's the adult's enthusiasm that sparks the child's interest.

Spontaneous worship is one of the most beautiful and

enriching experiences a child can have at church or home. Pausing in a moment of awe and wonder to breathe a quick prayer of gratitude is an effective way for an adult to lead a child in thankfulness to God. When the child is wide-eyed over the colors of a butterfly wing, the teacher can express his own feelings of reverence, providing a model for the child to follow in his own reactions. It would be presumptuous to label the child's response the same as the adult's, since outer expressions are often inadequate in revealing inner feelings. But these moments of interest and wonder that come through the child's discoveries of God's world are far more meaningful than the routine forms of worship in surroundings far beyond the child's level of understanding.

Most important of all, the impact of the child's experiences at church depends on the quality of the relationships with people there. The church that is concerned for its children to feel loved must provide understanding and patient adults who sincerely love each child. Personal attention from sensitive adults, plus pleasant interaction with other children, add the human element that is so essential to Christian nurture and development. These adults also become visible representations to the child of what God is like, an awesome, but thrilling responsibility for all those who guide young children.

Notes

1. Goldman, *Religious Thinking from Childhood to Adolescence,* p. 199.
2. David Elkind, "The Child's Conception of His Religious Denomination: The Protestant Child," in *The Journal of Genetic Psychology,* 1963, vol. 103, pp. 291-304.
3. Goldman, *Religious Thinking from Childhood to Adolescence,* p. 194.

CHAPTER FIVE

The Child, the Bible and Prayer

"I don't think I like God."

"Why?"

"Because it says she (the child identified herself with the 'I' of the Twenty-third Psalm) doesn't want Him."

"But that means He won't let the person want for anything he needs."

"But He makes her lie down on the ground."

"You would like that if you were a sheep."

"I don't want to be a sheep."

THE CHILD AND THE BIBLE

This five-year-old had earned the praise and admiration of her parents and teachers for memorizing the Twenty-third Psalm. Her performance had been all that adults could ask of a child's recitation, spoken with every evidence of assurance and understanding. And then, almost as an afterthought, she said, "I don't think I like God." She had succeeded from all outward appearances, but the sense she made of the Scripture passage was something totally different from what the adults assumed.

The Bible and prayer are aspects of Christian life which the child can encounter directly. Yet they are often shrouded with intrigue and mystery. The child is told that through the Bible God speaks directly to him, and through prayer he can personally address God. As in the case of the little girl and the Twenty-third Psalm, understanding these concepts presents difficulties for the child's developing thought process.

Most young children have positive feelings about the Bible, even though they understand so very little of it.[1] They have been told it is important. And they accept the judgment of the adults in their lives. However, symbolic terms, such as "lamp," "sword," and "bread," made in reference to the Bible, misguide a child's literal thinking. Often a child selects some nonessential factor as the Bible's distinguishing mark. The Bible's physical appearance, its age, its adult language, its use in church seem to a child as the unique quality that makes it such a significant book. He has no comprehension of its construction, other than a vague notion that God wrote it. Because it is the vehicle through which Christian concepts are communicated to the child, the misconceptions that grow out of its presentation can affect many other of his concepts and feelings.

One problem in using the Bible with young children grows out of efforts to teach the child about the Bible as an isolated subject. Adults often seem compelled to impress a child with the importance of certain information. Thus, Bible stories and statements are often prefaced with comments designed to make the child take special note of what is being said. In most cases it would probably be just as effective to merely state that the incident really happened, and let the Bible story stand on its own merits. To do more than that often clouds the issue by making the people and events seem so unique that the child cannot identify with them.

For example, in a kindergarten department one of the teachers had just returned from a trip to Israel. She wanted to help the children visualize the scenes where many of the Bible stories occurred. So, she displayed photographs she had taken there. Much to her surprise, the most interesting fact for the children was simply the ideas that she had been able to physically go to those places. Many of the children found it very hard to believe that the Bible stories had occurred at real places. As one little boy expressed it, "You can't go to Bethlehem. It's in heaven." Teacher's efforts to impress children with the Bible's sacred character resulted in removing the stories from the child's understanding of physical reality.

Historical-cultural gap

In terms of the actual biblical content, a major barrier to understanding by the young child is the immense historical and cultural gap that exists between the limited experience of the modern child and the events of biblical narrative. When most children under six have difficulty understanding recent events, asking them to develop accurate mental pictures of biblical events is a very tall order. The child, whose thought patterns naturally center on himself, assumes that everyone else lives as he does. He also is convinced others view all situations with the same perspective. Sometimes attempts to explain some of the critical differences in modes of living, acting and thinking often add to the problem, for the child is likely to twist the information to fit his view of life.

For example, many Bible stories that take place around a well lose much of their significance to a child who cannot visualize an alternative to modern plumbing. Some families of the Bible may seem somewhat unreal to the child whose entire family experience is restricted to modern America's pattern of few children, working mothers, and absent fathers. The sacrificial worship at the Tabernacle or Temple is totally foreign to the background of today's child. And what impression does a four-year-old receive from the Old Testament battle narratives?

Compounding the culture separation is the inability of the child to understand the sequence of time. For the child who gathers all his past memories under the vague umbrella term of "yesterday," or "last night," the scope of biblical chronology is hopelessly complex. To the child who is dominated by the present and has only dim awareness of his own years since babyhood, may find it difficult to think of Jesus as infant, boy and man. The little boy who envisioned baby Moses leading the Israelites across the Red Sea in baskets woven by their mothers was using all his mental powers to make all his pieces of information fit.

Vocabulary

Another difficulty for the young child is the vocabulary

of the Bible. Biblical names, for example, often make the characters appear very strange to the child. Also, the archaic wording of *King James Bible* English tends to make people and events obscure. Many words that are essential to biblical narrative and meaning often are grossly misunderstood by a child.

A teacher was telling her group of five-year-olds the story of the Good Samaritan. To encourage participation from these members of the "Sesame Street" generation, she asked if they knew what robbers were. Every hand went up, for they had all heard the term many times. But not one child gave the right answer. The teacher was startled, for "robbers" was hardly one of the more difficult words in the story. Yet, none of her children understood the term. They missed much of the story's meaning.

Such misunderstandings lead to another problem—the facility with which children can seem to understand and yet miss the whole point. Mere survival in a world that is far beyond their ability to comprehend seems to force the child into developing the skill of acting as if he knows what is going on when he really does not. Group singing illustrates this point. Each child may appear to be contributing with gusto to what sounds like a well-vocalized piece of music. Isolation of any one singer, however, often produces a strange outpouring of sense and nonsense. When the child did not know the words, he simply filled in with noise that sounded like what everyone else was singing. The amazing thing is that the child sings the gibberish with the same confidence as he sings the words, totally oblivious to its lack of meaning.

In the area of Christian concepts this misunderstanding is a serious problem. The child, unable to understand the meaning of a word, phrase or idea yet unaware that he misunderstands, answers with words he has heard adults or an older child express. Parents and teachers show pleasure at hearing the child mouth the proper arrangement of words. They seldom press further to discover what meaning those words really possess for the child.

Memorization

Rote memorization is another aspect that often compounds the child's difficulty in understanding Scripture. Zealous adults strive to have the child commit to memory something that "he will understand later on." Or, they assume he understands since for them the meaning is obvious. The child says the words. The proud parents beam. However, the child may have no adequate understanding. Words, phrases and ideas that are unrelated to the child's present experience have little immediate or long-range significance for him.[2] The effort expended on recitation could be far more profitably expended on activities (such as those suggested in the Activity section of this chapter) in which biblical statements are used repeatedly, but in direct relation to a specific activity in which the child is engaged.

Symbolism

Symbolism presents another difficulty in the young child's understanding of Bible content. Many biblical concepts are presented in terms of imagery and allegories which carry great impact for adults, but result in confusion for the child. His thinking is dominated by his literal concept of words. For the young child who is wrestling with his own developing self-concept, the idea of being something other than what he obviously is looms as most unpleasant, often truly unthinkable. While he may enjoy pretending to be something else, his fun is due to his recognition that he is not something else. It is only make-believe.

The child's very literal use of words represents his great difficulty in handling symbolism. He cannot think beyond the literal symbol to perceive the rich meaning that it is intended to portray.[3] Since the Bible frequently uses symbolism to convey an idea, the child faces a great problem in understanding, but a problem that he does not know is there.

For example, many of Jesus' parables, which are truly superb examples of teaching through symbolism, will be misunderstood by young children. While they may enjoy hearing about the Lost Sheep, the Lost Coin, the Mustard Seed, or the Sower and the Seed, they may view them as merely interesting stories about sheep, coins and seeds.

Efforts to apply the concept of these kinds of stories to the life experiences of children prove very difficult. Older children even have problems in taking an idea from one setting and using it in another situation. The very straightforward narrative of the parable of the Good Samaritan, which clearly illustrates one person helping another person in need, was frequently misinterpreted by eleven- and twelve-year-olds who were attempting to apply its teaching to another set of circumstances.[4] How much more difficult is this task with children under six?

Miracles

The Bible's miracles often pose difficulty for the young child's comprehension. The problem is not one of belief, for the child readily accepts the miraculous. The problem is one of practice. For example, a Sunday School teacher was telling her four-year-olds about some children who were very disappointed because a promised picnic had been rained out. She asked her class what those children could possibly do that would be better than fussing about this setback. The unanimous conclusion was that the children should pray, asking God to stop the rain. And one little boy added, "Just like Jesus did in the boat."

The child thinks very logically that if God loves him and has all that power, He should be willing to expend it to solve a current problem. And since the child is convinced that nothing is more important than the immediate present, he expects God to feel the same way. The child tends to view the miraculous as expected everyday occurrences, since he has so little understanding of the cause and effect relationships in his world. The operation of an automobile engine is as much a mystery to him as the parting of the Red Sea. He thus has a very difficult time drawing a workable line between the natural and supernatural. When a child hears a story of a biblical miracle he accepts it uncritically along with all the other remarkable things in his world that seem to happen so amazingly.

The important thing for a child to understand about a Bible story involving a miracle is the purpose for God's action. Stories of a physical healing, for example, can be used effectively to show Jesus' love for an individual. "Jesus helped the blind man to see because He loved him," is a logical and meaningful explanation a child can grasp.

"Jesus loved His friends. Jesus didn't want His friends to be afraid. He helped them by stopping the storm." This emphasis focuses the child's attention on Jesus' deed. Not as an end in itself, but as a way to show love and compassion to friends in need.

The significance of these difficulties

It is very difficult to measure the impact on the child of these difficulties in understanding biblical content. It is presumptuous to expect a beginning student in any subject to start with a mature concept of that subject. To find a childish misconception about a Bible story is no more surprising than to find childish errors in spelling and arithmetic. These errors are actually key building blocks in the learning process. As errors become evident, patient and loving adults can guide the child in ways that will help clarify his understanding of Bible truths.

However, this process does not often happen in dealing with the Bible. Adults tend to assume that the child's interest in Bible stories indicates that the child has adequately understood the significance of the stories. Thus the child is allowed to continue thinking he knows what a given story was all about, when in fact he has often totally missed the point.

Many such evidences are seen with older children and adolescents who rebel at efforts to deal with familiar biblical narratives because, "I know that story already!" If the objective for teaching Bible content was simply to have people know the factual account of stories, then that complaint would very often be justified. Unfortunately, that is precisely the way in which biblical material is often presented by parents and teachers. However, if the purpose for teaching biblical content to children is to help them learn more than mere facts, then the situation is considerably more complex.

Parents and teachers should have a clear objective in mind before introducing children to Bible narratives. The child needs to begin to learn Bible content in ways that will influence his thinking, feeling and actions. It is especially important that this Bible material be presented in a simple and clear manner, appropriate to the child's learning level. For when a child misunderstands something the Bible says, the result can frequently be the development of a negative attitude toward God, as well as to other spiritual concepts. While it is often possible to correct a faulty piece of information by giving a better answer, attitudes are much more difficult to change. Thus, feelings often continue long after the knowledge that originally created that feeling has been corrected. Fortunately, most children feel positively about God, even though their level of understanding is indeed immature. This positive feeling can be given a more solid base, however, by the appropriate use of biblical material.

The impact of Bible stories on children's behavior raises some important questions, also. Investigations have repeatedly shown little or no connection between a child's knowledge of the Bible and the way in which he feels or acts. These findings can be explained by understanding the child's great difficulty in making the transfer of learning from one situation to another. Simple knowledge of the facts of a story is not enough to have a significant impact on the child to affect his own behavior. Even getting the child to say what kind of behavior he should follow is no guarantee that he will follow his own advice.[5]

This problem is by no means limited to early childhood. It has been the dilemma of moral educators of all time—how to get people to actually do what they know they should. Christianity has presented only one effective answer—a spiritual rebirth through acceptance of Jesus Christ as Saviour and Lord. (See chapter 6.) There are specific steps that parents and teachers can take to prepare a child for making this meaningful spiritual commitment. These steps involve helping the child to discover for himself the joy of living in accord with biblical principles.

ACTIVITIES FOR LEARNING ABOUT THE BIBLE

Few things communicate the significance of God's Word more effectively to a young child than the attitudes and actions of the adults in his life. When a child sees his parents, for instance, reading and studying the Bible, when he hears them talk about God's Word as it relates to their everyday experiences and when he senses their dependence upon the Bible as their chief source of inspiration, then he, too, will be learning to value God's Word. Adults who show by the healthy vigor of their way of living, that practicing biblical teachings is a way to show love for the Lord, will provide children with an attractive model worth emulating. God's Word demonstrated is more convincing than God's Word explained!

THE BIBLE STORY

Adults need to carefully consider which sections of the Bible to use with young children. Since the Bible is a book written for adults, a great deal of its content is inappropriate for a child. Much of the Old Testament prophecies and the New Testament epistles would be both uninteresting and unintelligible to little ones.

In selecting those parts of Scripture that will be meaningful to children, parents and teachers should look for stories that contain elements familiar to the child's experience. The closer the actions of story characters are to situations the child has encountered, the more likely he will be to connect the example with his own behavior.

A key aspect in the effectiveness of any story is the degree to which the child can identify with a person in the narrative.[6]

The stories of young Samuel assisting in the Tabernacle or of David give models of children who accepted and carried out responsibility successfully. Samuel's situation deserves a word of caution, however. The account of his mother dedicating him to God and taking him to live with the priests can arouse strong negative feelings in some children who fear being abandoned.

Old Testament stories about the construction, care or repair of the Tabernacle or Temple can be useful in helping a child to feel responsibility for his own church. Stress the specific things people did to express their respect for the place of worship. Minimize the unique aspects of sacrificial observances.

Children respond positively to the stories of Jesus' birth and boyhood. They quickly identify with baby Jesus, for here is a person close to their own life experiences. The care of Mary and Joseph for the baby touches responsive chords in children.

The story about Jesus and the children has always been a favorite. Each child can imagine Jesus picking him up and smiling directly at him. This story is very effective in helping children develop warm feelings towards Jesus, especially when they sense He is on their side, and not with those stuffy, unfriendly adults.

Zacchaeus is a very appealing character to young children despite his unsavory reputation. They admire his ingenuity to climb a tree in an effort to see over the big people, certainly a familiar problem to little ones. Jesus' recognition of Zacchaeus and His willingness to forgive his wrongdoing completes the intrigue of this narration. For each child has his own memories of unacceptable actions. The assurance of forgiveness at this story's conclusion helps children feel positively about Jesus' consideration for Zacchaeus.

Jesus' triumphant entry into Jerusalem can be used to help children express their feelings of love to Jesus. Conclude this account of Bible times by suggesting children sing glad songs to Him to show their love.

The New Testament accounts of ways Christians helped one another carry a clear message children can understand.

TELLING THE BIBLE STORY

Activities

It is not enough to find a Bible story with which the child can easily identify. The desired transfer to his behavior takes place only if the story is definitely related to real-life experiences. Making this transfer verbally has not proved entirely successful. The child may be able to talk about the point of the story without putting it into effect. A more successful approach is to use the story while the child is involved in a real-life situation.

Sunday School teachers can help to accomplish this transfer of learning through activities in the various learning centers. For example, several children may be playing with blocks, building a rocket ship. The teacher can use conversation about the rocket for a brief account of the creation story from Genesis. Helping the child to see that the Bible says that God created the earth, the moon and the stars, connects Bible facts with the physical activity of the children.

When Alice gave Sharon a turn to rock the doll at the home living area, the teacher nearby commented, "Alice, you are a kind friend to Sharon when you let her use the doll for a while. I know a story about a young man who made someone very happy, just like you did. Would you like to hear that story?" How could Alice resist? The teacher proceeded to tell both girls about Paul, who wrote to his young friend Timothy asking him to bring his books and his coat. The girls who had just experienced what it means to help someone, joined in an animated discussion of how Paul must have felt when Timothy arrived. They were also interested in talking of how Timothy felt when he saw how pleased his friend was to see him. The close relationship between the Bible story and the children's actual experience made this a good learning opportunity.

Teachers often have to arrange such circumstances to

provide real-life experiences within the classroom. The parent, however, has the distinct advantage of living with the child in a host of everyday situations. When parents are alert to opportunities to relate Bible stories and truths to the things the child really does, the story can be a good means of instruction. "What you did reminds me of a story in the Bible. . . ." is an effective use of these stories as positive reinforcement for desirable behavior.

Visuals

Presenting a Bible story is often enhanced by the use of visual techniques. Pictures of the characters in the story help a child visualize them and think of them as real people. Have a Bible with attractive Bible story pictures in it, since a child's interest in any book depends to a great extent on its illustrations. Use a picture of a present-day situation that corresponds with a child's personal experiences to provide a basis for conversation in connection with Bible story action.

After a teacher told the story of the Good Samaritan she showed the children a picture of a little girl who had fallen off her tricycle and scraped her knee. The picture also showed an older boy who had evidently been playing nearby coming to her side. The teacher asked the children to describe what was happening in the picture. They vividly and accurately told what they saw occurring.

The teacher then asked them to tell what they thought had happened before. These comments became less descriptive and more of a projection of their own feelings and experiences.

Then the teacher asked what they thought would happen next. By this time most of the children had firmly identified themselves with one of the two characters. One boy stated, much to everyone's consternation, that the boy in the picture was now going to take the little girl's tricycle away from her and ride it himself!

"Would that be better than helping the little girl go inside and get her knee fixed?" asked the teacher.

"Yes, 'cause then he could ride and have a lot of fun," declared the boy.

"How do you think he would feel?"

"He would feel real good, 'cause he was. . . , no, he'd feel kinda bad 'cause the little girl was still hurt."

"What do you think would make him feel the best?"

"If he helped her get her knee fixed."

Drama

Simple dramatic portrayal of Bible story action also helps a child connect a story to his own world. Story play, puppets, or even viewing filmstrips can make the incident much more real.

A group of five-year-olds was going to act out the story of the men who cut a hole in the roof to lower a sick man down to Jesus. The teacher gave effective guidance to their efforts. She asked questions such as, "How do you think the men felt while they were doing this?" Simple props and a great deal of imagination made the scene live for a few brief moments, even though the dialogue was inadequate according to adult standards. At the conclusion, the "sick man" got off his mat and looked "Jesus" in the eye. After saying "Thanks," he looked at the four who had carried him and announced, "Those guys are my friends." That young child obviously got the impact of the story!

"Tell it again!" are familiar words to those who work with young children. By all means, tell it again. Enhance the story by telling (or reading) it with enthusiasm, which is no easy order on the thirty-fifth retelling. Just watch the reaction of the child to the story's progress. He is thoroughly delighted partly because he can identify with the characters and their actions; also because he knows the sequence of events.

Expression

The most essential ingredient in story telling is the adult's enthusiasm! Express feelings of the story in your voice and actions. For instance, look angry or frightened. Yawn to express time for sleep. Smile a big smile to show happiness. Young children quickly sense and reflect these familiar feelings.

Questions

Questions, both about the story and about related experiences of the child also add a rich dimension, making each telling more meaningful.

After you've told a story, ask simple questions to help children recall the facts of the story. If a child flounders, give additional clues so he can answer correctly. Kindergartners will enjoy questions pertaining to the sequence of events in the story. Also, ask questions which require reasoning. "Why did Jesus help the sick boy to be well again?" Keep these questions simple. Give assistance by helping the child put his thoughts into words. Children enjoy answering questions that reflect their reaction to the story. "What part of the story did you like best?" Since there is no correct answer, the child feels "safe" to offer his feelings.

Bible memorization

Young children are remarkably adept at repeating what they hear. Reciting Bible verses learned by rote however, has little significance for a child if he does not understand the meaning. To help him know the meaning of Bible words, relate them to a real situation. When a child hears Galatians 6:10 (*TLB*), for instance, spoken at a time when he is being kind to someone, he will relate those words to his actions: "David, when you helped Lisa pick up the puzzle pieces she dropped, you were doing just what the Bible says. The Bible says, 'Always be kind to everyone.' "

Showing the child pictures of people being kind, as you help him recall times when he experienced kindness, adds to his understanding. Commending him for his acts of kindness also reinforces the desired behavior attractive to him. Again and again with conversation, songs, explanations and pictures, build for the child a groundwork of familiarity with understanding. Memorization may accompany these experiences, but is not the aim.

THE CHILD AND PRAYER

"Dear God, thank you for my mother and daddy and for Carol and Don and for Tippy. Help me be a good helper when we mow the lawn tomorrow."

Billy's prayer demonstrated a young child's amazing

sense of the reality of God. He may express his concern for all the important people in his life by listing them in his prayer, or he may offer a catalog of all the good things he wants for himself. He enjoys prayer for it gives him a sense of security and of mastery. The security comes from a sense that God hears him and will make sure that all goes well. Mastery is the feeling that comes from being able to talk directly to Someone important, knowing He will do what he wants Him to do.

However, the child has little awareness of what prayer really is.[7] Jeffrey, aged four, talked of his prayers as being literal things: "And then the wind comes and blows them up to heaven where God is." Anna, aged five, believed that failure to get the expected answer was due to faulty transmission on her part. "You have to know the right words to make them (prayers) work."

These are very common kinds of statements that children make about prayer, and they illustrate the twin dilemma caused by the child's vague notions of what prayer is, coupled with a strong certainty that his notion is correct. The child's ideas about prayer are highly colored by his ideas of God, depending to a great extent on what he believes God to be like.

The child's prayer also reflects his childish level of thought. The great proportion of prayers by children are naturally self-centered, since the basic outlook of the child is egocentric. Even when he prays for others, it is often phrased in terms of that person's relationship to himself. For example, five-year-old Dina prayed, "And please help Mommy and Daddy to love me." Since a loving relationship is the most pleasant way of life for Dina, the prayer is very natural. She is not yet fully aware of her parents as people separate from her, who do things that have no relationship to her. That will come after a few more years of family living.

Most children enjoy using memorized prayers at times. The rhyme and rhythm of many of these appeal to children. Recitation also provides the satisfaction that they are praying just like someone else, which is very reassuring at times. However, the memorized prayer tends to be rattled off with little thought to meaning. Also, these kinds of prayers are sometimes used to cover adult embarrassment over not feeling at ease in spontaneous prayer expressions. Obviously, much of the child's feelings, thoughts and practice concerning prayer will be determined by the adult models which he observes.

ACTIVITIES FOR LEARNING ABOUT PRAYER

To catch the spirit of prayer, a child needs repeated opportunities to hear the adults in his life pray. Your attitude of reverence and sincerity is keenly felt by a child. While he may not understand all the words, he senses that talking to God is a very real experience. When he consistently hears your expressions of thanksgiving and praise to God for His loving care, His gifts and His forgiveness, the child soon begins to recognize that God is loving and cares about people, including himself.

When teachers or parents express their own feelings in a very real firsthand experience, the child is being given an appropriate model for expressing his own responses. Prayer is then not merely a formula, it is an expression of real feelings.

For example, Richy's family vacation was unexpectedly cut short by an urgent business crisis. Richy heard his dad pray, "Lord, you know how disappointed we are about having to go home now. We are really unhappy. Please help us to remember the good times we had this week and to be glad for them." The drive home was spent in reminiscing about the enjoyments of their week.

Many parents find that bedtime becomes a much more pleasant time of day for all concerned when it is used to recall the happy things of the day. Following a relaxed conversation about the favorite experiences of both child and parent, Mom or Dad may simply say, "Dear God, I am so thankful for the good time we had at dinner tonight. We enjoyed the food and being together was such fun. Thank you for my wonderful family." The child can then be asked if there is something he would like to thank God for.

Bedtime can also be a very effective time to clear the air of unpleasant feelings caused by family conflicts. Take care in these situations to avoid using prayers to preach to the child. Praying that God will help Billy not to be such a stinker tomorrow can only serve to build resistance in the child.

One mother wisely prayed after a particularly trying evening, "Father, I am sorry I let myself get so upset with Brian today. Help me to be more patient." Nothing was said that Brian should also pray similarly. But several months later, after hearing similar kinds of confessions and requests for help from his parents, he closed his prayer with the postscript: "And Jesus, I think I was too fussy today. Help me to be nicer tomorrow."

Parents often teach their very young child an easily

memorized prayer poem as his first way to talk to God. However, just as they buy larger clothes as their child grows, so they also need to provide him with the opportunity to move beyond the rote prayers of his younger years.

Sometimes it is helpful for teachers in the church school (or parents at home) to have a child repeat phrase by phrase the prayer you pray. This experience is a first step toward the child's using his own words. Keep your prayer short. Avoid symbolism or flowery expressions! Children do not comprehend these figures of speech. For a prayer to be meaningful, a child should understand what he is saying. Talk to the Lord about things within the children's experience. Speak naturally. Avoid using archaic terms, such as *thy, thou* and *thee.*

As a child's language skills increase, it is easier for him to express his feelings in his own words. However, he needs guidance in focusing his thoughts. "Thank you, God, for all my blessings," encompasses more than a young child's mind can grasp! To center his thinking, ask simple questions to help him discover a specific way God cares for him. "Karen, what did you eat for breakfast this morning? . . . Who cooked your cereal? (Combed your hair? polished your shoes? brought you home from church?) What other ways do your mother and daddy help you? . . . God planned for you to have a family! Let's thank God for the ones He planned to love and care for us. If you would like to say, 'Thank you, God, for my family,' you may come and stand by me while we pray." Conclude prayer, "Dear God, we thank you for the families of boys and girls here today. We are glad you love each one of us.

We love you. In Jesus' name, Amen." This type of participation may help a child who is reticent about praying aloud to feel a part of your prayer.

Of course teachers will be alert to any child in their group whose family is composed of other than the traditional members, such as foster or grandparents, aunts, etc. Assure the child that, "Mrs. Davis is your family. God planned for her to take care of you."

To respond in heartfelt thanks to God, a child should be aware of specific ways God provides for his needs. This awareness of God's loving care is often his first step toward expressing feelings of gratitude. In your daily routine, call your child's attention to items that he can see, smell, taste, touch and hear; relate the experience to God's care for him. For instance, as you pour his juice, say, "God made oranges so you can drink this good-tasting juice. Isn't God good to you! Let's thank God for this juice."

To help children know they can help others by praying for them, gather pictures of your missionary, your pastor and several teachers in your department. Talk with the children about ways each of these people help others learn of the Lord. Use words children understand.

When a child prays in his own words, never let him flounder. Simply ask, "Would you like me to help you think of words you want to say to God?" Avoid making him feel his prayer is wrong or poorly expressed.

During the Bible learning activity part of your morning schedule, you'll discover many opportunities to guide a child in a brief prayer. During these informal moments when a child is ready and perhaps even eager to pray, he often needs you to provide a simple prayer statement he can repeat. For instance, as a child arranges a bouquet of flowers, ask simple questions to help him be aware of the flowers' color, fragrance and unique shape. When you sense his feelings of wonder and awe (which is often a reflection of your own), quietly say, "Sharon, we can thank God for making these flowers for us." If the child seems unsure of what to say, you can suggest, "You can say 'Thank you, God, for these flowers.' "

As a child works with his hands (cutting, drawing, painting), say, "Janet, just look at the interesting work your hands can do! What did God make for you so you can hold scissors? . . . For what other things do you need your fingers? . . . Let's thank God right now for your fingers. You can say, 'Thank you, God, for my fingers.' "

Kindergartners will be interested in knowing that the Lord's Prayer is a prayer Jesus taught and that it is recorded in our Bible. However, the phrases are long and many of the words are beyond the understanding of a young child. ("Give us this day our jelly bread," one child prayed.) When a child is elementary age, learning and memorizing this significant part of Scripture will be a more meaningful experience than during these years of early childhood. In group settings avoid putting children on the spot for a prayer "performance." Praying in front of others may cause a child to focus his attention on the group, not on God.

When we spend time each day talking with God, when we turn first to Him in an anxious moment, when our thinking and our plans reflect our dependence upon His guidance, then the children will likely sense through our attitude and actions the reality of prayer in our own life.

Our task is to earnestly share with the children our deep belief in prayer. Then the result of our work is in the hands of the Holy Spirit.

Notes

1. M. B. Evans, *Religious Ideas and Attitudes of the Young Child,* Unpublished doctoral dissertation, Wayne State University, 1964.
2. Munsinger, *Fundamentals of Child Development,* p. 124.
3. Goldman, *Religious Thinking from Childhood to Adolescence,* p. 21.
4. J. G. Kenwrick, *The Religious Quest* (London: S.P.C.K., 1955), p. 23.
5. Munsinger, *Fundamentals of Child Development,* p. 205.
6. Eleanor Zimmerman, *Doctrine for 3's to 5's* (Philadelphia: Lutheran Church Press, 1963), p. 49.
7. D. Long, D. Elkind, and B. Spilka, "The Child's Conception of Prayer," in *Journal for the Scientific Study of Religion,* 1967, vol. 6, pp. 102-108.

CHAPTER SIX

The Child and Jesus

"Why did Jesus live on earth?"

"God wanted people to know He loved them and some couldn't hear His inside whisper, so He sent Jesus to tell them out loud."[1]

This answer by a five-year-old boy is very perceptive. It recognizes the basic purpose of the Incarnation and the existence of a special relationship between Jesus and God the Father. This doctrine has mystified theologians for nearly two thousand years, let alone five-year-olds.

Who was the Man, Jesus Christ? What was the nature of His relationship with the Father? How was He similar to and different from any other man? Where is He now, and what is His present role? These questions studied by scholars, preachers and laymen since the time of Christ are at the very core of Christianity. They are also similar to the kinds of questions a young child asks about Jesus: Who was Jesus? Is God Jesus' daddy? Was Jesus a little baby or a big man? Where is Jesus now? The answers children give to their own questions are not always as mature as the one given at the beginning of this chapter. Children's responses do, however, often show the beginnings of insight into the concept of Jesus.

JESUS AND GOD

The most frequent problem that investigators, teachers and parents have found in the child's thinking about Jesus is the overwhelming tendency to confuse Jesus and God.[2] Most children under six will use the two names interchangeably. Ask a child, "Who made the world?" and he is as likely to name Jesus as creator as he is to answer that God made everything. Show him a picture of Jesus and ask him who it is. Either reply can be expected.

An adult's attempt to clarify the child's view often serves only to increase the difficulty. Efforts to emphasize the distinctions between Jesus and God run the risk of creating two Gods in the child's mind. Since the overlapping of Jesus and God has a solid backing in biblical teaching, it should not be viewed as a total error, but rather as an incomplete understanding.

ATTRACTIVENESS OF JESUS

Another aspect of the young child's thoughts of Jesus is a very strong attraction that most youngsters exhibit towards Him. Generally, children who have had any exposure to stories about Jesus feel that He is warm, sympathetic and pleasant. Rarely does a young child express feelings of antagonism towards Jesus, in contrast to occasional outbursts that a child may direct against God, teachers or parents. The reason for these almost unanimous good feelings seems to be that the stories and songs the child hears about Him are almost exclusively of a loving, supportive nature. Judgmental or punishment references are generally portrayed in terms of God, the Father. Also, the child identifies very strongly with the concept of baby Jesus and the concept of Him as God's Son, therefore making Him the child's ally against an adult dominated and sometimes hostile world.

DEATH AND RESURRECTION

Psychologists who have investigated the young child's view of death have found that children in our society under the age of six have very vague notions of what death involves. Not until the age of five or six does the child view death as permanent, but sees it merely as another form of separation.[3] Children often expect physical resurrections of dead birds, pets and grandparents. Thus the resurrection of Jesus is seen as very normal, not at all extraordinary. In our society children are insulated from death. They rarely feel the loss of anyone within their immediate family. The young child has little difficulty accepting the facts of the Resurrection, since he really does not comprehend the meaning of death. The emphasis for the child should be "Jesus is living, and we are glad!"

SALVATION

A sensitive area in the thinking of those concerned with a child's Christian education is the question of the child's salvation. Mainstream Christianity has consistently maintained that the focal issue of any person's spiritual life is the question of his personal relationship to Jesus Christ. A definite individual commitment to follow Christ as example and Lord, based on acceptance of His sacrificial death, is proclaimed by the church as man's only means of finding eternal life. Many Christians have thus advocated seeking to lead children into that commitment as early in their lives as possible. How early in life is it really possible for a person to properly make this commitment? Some people suggest children as young as two are ready; others maintain any decision made before adolescence is suspect. Much of the disagreement is based in opposing theological views of the spiritual status of the infant. Is he born innocent or is he already tainted by original sin? However, most of the attention seems to be focused on determining the age at which the child can really be considered to be held accountable for his actions and his decisions. Perhaps the mental and emotional age rather than the chronological age of the child is the determining factor.

There are some very real problems involved in applying the principle of accountability to children under six. In order for a child to be considered guilty of sin, and thus in need of cleansing and forgiveness, the child must be able to understand the significance of his actions. More is involved than his merely recognizing that certain actions are acceptable and others are not. The decision demands that the child be capable of accepting responsibility for his acts and their consequences.

This is a critical point, for there are very few areas of life in which a child under six is generally capable of personal responsibility. Is he allowed to settle the question of whether or not he will attend kindergarten? Is he considered mature enough to decide whether or not to brush his teeth? Is a visit to the doctor within his realm of choice? He may be allowed to choose the color of shirt he will wear today, the flavor of ice cream he wants to eat, or the games he will play with his friends. Can it be expected that these experiences give him enough background in making choices to enable him to make so momentous a decision?

The fact that a young child is easily manipulated further complicates the issue. He succumbs to the right kind of pressure. Most young children keenly desire to please the significant adults in their lives. They endure innumerable inconveniences to earn a smile, a pat, or a word of commendation. Recognition from adults is one of the strongest motivators in the young child's experience. The parent or teacher who asks the child, "Would you like to ask Jesus to forgive your sins?" is more likely to have the child respond out of a desire to cooperate than from a true conviction or understanding of what is happening.

A desire to do what other children are doing is also a powerful factor in leading many children to announce their intention to become a Christian. While many children are very adept at displaying their will, often with fierce stubbornness, the specific issue at any one time is very much a product of that moment. It is not the result of careful planning and evaluation by the child. Every parent and teacher utilizes the very effective tactic of changing the child's unacceptable behavior by substituting another attraction to draw his interest. What a child considers a matter of life and death one moment is totally forgotten the next. Also, a child's perceptive question may lead an adult to think the youngster is all primed for some significant information. Actually, attention quickly followed another path, leaving the helpful adult in mid explanation.

Repentance is another issue of importance, for it is frequently mentioned in the Bible as a necessary ingredient of salvation. While a child may express sorrow for a specific misdeed, it is highly questionable that his sorrow is more than distress resulting from his unpleasant behavior. The young child's inability to think in general terms makes it very difficult for him to ask forgiveness and cleansing for sin as a broad category. Childish thought processes greatly limit comprehension of the repentance aspect of the salvation experience.

The analysis is, of course, limited to a human perspective. The process of regeneration is in many ways beyond the realm of human understanding. The exact way in which the Holy Spirit works to draw a person to God remains a mystery. Testimonials of parents, teachers and ultimately of the individuals themselves, give support to the spiritual encounters by children under six. The child raised in a supportive, Christian environment may express a desire to accept Jesus into his life. Sensitive questioning and an openness to the Spirit's guidance can guide parents and teachers to know how to respond. (See *Guiding the young child toward Jesus* in this chapter.)

ACTIVITIES FOR LEARNING ABOUT JESUS

A basic rule of thumb for helping children begin to know about Jesus is to place the major emphasis on His humanity. When we introduce Jesus from the perspective of His deity we make the child's learning task far more complex. Jesus recognized this problem Himself as He taught His disciples and other followers. He called them to follow Him, to observe and learn from Him. Only gradually did they come to see Him as the Son of God. And then, evidently, as the result of a special revelation to Peter. (See Matt. 16:16,17.)

Similarly, it is best to allow the child's natural attraction to the person of Jesus to draw him closer to the Master. With that type of foundation, evidence of Jesus' divine nature will take on more significance for the child as his concepts mature.

Relating Jesus' life to the child's experience

Jesus' infancy and boyhood are of special interest to children. While the Bible relates very little of these early years, it does clearly state that young Jesus "kept increasing in wisdom and stature, and in favor with God and men" (Luke 2:52). Children's fascination with the process of growth, especially their own transformation from infancy to childhood, helps children to identify with Jesus. Also, talking about ways Jesus grew helps to alleviate some of the uncertainty about whether He was a baby or a man. Many children have seen Him only in those two stages of life and need to see Him also as a growing boy.

To make Jesus' boyhood meaningful to the child, relate it to some of the child's firsthand experience. Comment about ways Jesus helped His family. Knowing that Jesus went to school and church are of real interest when compared to the child's own experiences.

Another facet of Jesus' life that is of keen interest to children is His work as a carpenter. Most four- and five-year-olds are capable of using small hammers and saws to construct rather amazing structures. Provide them with some soft wood, roofing nails and a place to work. Of course, some preliminary instruction and a bit of understanding guidance are necessary for safety. What better setting could there be, then, for an informal discussion about the kinds of things Jesus might have made in His carpentry shop. This activity also provides opportunity to talk about the strength and skill required to build with wood. This kind of conversation helps children to see Jesus as a strong and capable man.

Children are interested to know that Jesus taught people many things about God. Teachers are very important people in the young child's life. This title is helpful to their understanding of Jesus. Help children to know specific ways Jesus helped people, both by what He said and what He did. Also, ways He avoided acting selfishly. Use these examples in a positive way. For example, "David, you were really kind to give Nancy a turn to ride your tricycle. I think that is just what Jesus would have done." It is also helpful for children to be aware that adults try to emulate Jesus' example. "I'll be glad to help you fix that truck, Danny. Jesus always helped people, and I want to be like Him."

However, if Jesus' example is held up to the child in an effort to prod him on to better efforts, it can take on the same tone as, "Why can't you be neat like your sister?"

Highly damaging to a child's self-concept! The child builds resentments toward what appears to him to be unattainable expectations. Thus, it is wise to avoid statements like, "Jesus wouldn't like that," or, "Don't you want to be like Jesus, Ronny?" This approach is likely to earn the response one mother got when she asked her three-year-old to help pick up her toys, "because we love Jesus." The little girl thought for a moment, then said, "You love Jesus, Mommy. You pick up the toys."

Talking about Jesus' actions will lead naturally into considering some of His miracles. The child has no difficulty accepting the reality of the miracles, only in applying that information to his own experience. Guide the conversation so the child understands Jesus did wonderful things to help people because He loved them. For the child the importance of these miraculous deeds is not the deeds themselves, but the purpose they served. "Jesus loved those men so much that He did not want them to be sick. He made them well because He loved them."

Often the child will have further questions about the details of a miracle. At this point, the adult should be willing to admit honestly to the child when he does not understand himself "how Jesus made the dead man to live again." None of the child's faith is destroyed by hearing an adult say, "This is one of the things about God that I still don't really understand. I hope I can find the answer someday."

Seeing pictures of Jesus helps the child to feel a closer relationship to Him. Of course, some child is bound to ask if Jesus really looked like that. This thought usually occurs to him after he has been exposed to several different pictures by different artists. Most children are satisfied to be told that the picture is merely what one artist thought Jesus looked like, since no one drew His picture when He was on earth.

Songs about Jesus are very effective in building children's concepts and feelings. Words set to melody become oft repeated and tend to become authoritative definitions for the child. "Jesus Loves Me" has long been a Sunday School staple that has had a powerful impact on children. (The words of the stanzas are generally not understood by children under six.) "Jesus Loves the Little Children" has effectively communicated the idea that Jesus loves children, although its interracial message gets blurred in the line, "Red and yellow, black and white." This enumerating generally comes across to a child as just a miscellaneous listing of different colors. Efforts to identify these colors with people's skin tones often meet firm resistance from children who are convinced that "Nobody has red skin!" The idea of people having yellow and white skin get the same reactions, even in groups populated with both oriental and caucasian children. The literal vocabulary of the child will often only let black stand as a genuine skin color, and even that will have its dissenters.

These examples provide a warning signal to adults to look at songs from a child's perspective. Decide if the message that comes across is the one that is intended. One teacher discovered, after trying to teach her five-year-olds to sing "Fairest Lord Jesus," that her children interpreted the first line to be a reference that Jesus did not cheat. The child's idea certainly did not fit with the song's intent to compare Jesus with the wonders of creation.

Relating Christmas and Easter to the child's experience

The two most significant times in the Christian year center around pivotal events in the life of Jesus. These Christian festivals have special attraction for children. Christmas and Easter pose real problems in teaching, however, both because of the great confusion between the religious and secular aspects of the occasions, as well as the challenge of communicating the significance of the original events in a way that children can understand.

Four-year-old Alan thought he had Easter analyzed when he explained that "it was when Jesus arose from the grave and the Easter bunny hopped out after Him."

There is no point in engaging in further handwringing over the way in which Christmas has become the most materialistic time of the year as we celebrate the birth of the man who said, "Do not lay up for yourselves treasures upon earth, . . . but seek first His kingdom, and His righteousness" (Matt. 6:19,33).

Sadly, most Christian families spend far more time and energy on the secular aspects of Christmas than on the spiritual, all the while muttering at how "society" has corrupted Christmas. Without diminishing the pleasure of Christmas as a family time and the joy of giving and receiving gifts (although the massive quantities of frivolous presents do tend to make a mockery of the spirit of Christmas), thoughtful steps can be taken to increase the spiritual significance of Christmas for children.

Again, the key is the attitude of the adults. If the spiritual quality of Christmas is not truly meaningful to parents or teachers, attempts to force children to attend to sober observances will be self-defeating. The child will take his cue primarily from those things that are of greatest interest to the adults in his life.

The crèche has long been used as a focus of interest during the Christmas season. Allow children to participate in assembling the manger scene. Give them opportunity to move the figures as the story is told. Many children frequently return to the crèche during the holidays to play with the figures, retelling the story as they do.

Many of the decorative pieces of Christmas originated as symbols of religious truth. It is a beautiful thing for a child to be introduced to the tree, the holly wreath, and the colored lights as something other than just colorful backdrops for mountains of presents. A book of Christmas customs can be a very enriching addition to any home or classroom, for adults as well as children.

One or more colorful picture books of the Christmas story should be used throughout the holidays. Bedtime for a week or so before Christmas can be built around reading parts of the story.

Television, which bombards the home with Santa Claus and never-ending sales pitches for gift ideas, also provides occasional opportunities for viewing dramatic portrayals of the Christmas story. Selective viewing, which should be a pattern in any home, can make television an asset rather than the liability it frequently is.

Emphasizing the birthday aspect of Christmas strikes a responsive note in children. A birthday party for Jesus may be a little difficult for children to appreciate when they cannot see the guest of honor. However, they certainly enjoy talking about what Mary and Joseph might have done for Jesus on His second or fifth birthday. Talk with children about their own birthdays to help them relate the growth of Jesus to their own experience.

When families enjoy a time of carol singing, they need to include "Away in a Manger" or a song the younger family members are learning at church. A fun thing for a family is to spend an evening writing some new carols. Using tunes familiar to the child, write new words to tell the Christmas story.

Another meaningful family experience involves giving gifts to others outside the family. A family council several weeks before Christmas can decide whom to surprise and what to give. Often the gift can be something the whole family can participate in making, such as baking cookies. If all the family cannot share in making the gift, decorating the wrapping paper can be a joint project. Gadget printing is a simple yet creative and colorful way in which even the youngsters can participate.[4] Then, as the presents are delivered, everyone can truly feel they have had a part in the project. Some families vary their projects from year to year, doing something for neighbors, a nearby rest home, an orphanage, or perhaps the children's Sunday School teachers. By including the children in the planning and the work of the project, those children can have a meaningful experience of giving without hoping to receive in return.

What can the Easter story mean to the young child who possesses a vague concept of death? In the weeks preceding Easter give the child some experiences with life and death. This can be done most simply with the life cycle of plants. Let your child observe seeds growing to maturity as well as seeing the death of a leaf or flower. Conversation about the death of a pet or a wild animal will be very helpful, leading the child towards an understanding of the physical finality of death. As in any other area of life, the child will absorb the attitude of the adult. Parents who are fearful of death and become nervous when it is discussed will arouse the same feelings in the child. If parents can talk about death calmly, and answer questions honestly, the child will accept it as a natural process.

Conversations about separation help the child to understand, rather than fear, the sorrow that usually surrounds death. All children have experienced the pangs of temporary separation from parents, thus they can begin to understand why people are often sad when a person dies. In talking about the reaction of Jesus' friends when He was crucified, one teacher explained that "Jesus' friends were very sad when Jesus died because they thought they would never see him again. Some of them even cried, for they loved Him very much. Can you imagine how very happy they were when they found out that Jesus wasn't dead anymore! They must have laughed, and hugged each other, and told all their friends, 'Jesus isn't dead. He is alive! Jesus is living!' "

At Easter emphasize the joy we feel because Jesus is living. While the simple facts of the Crucifixion story can be told, avoid the gruesome aspects. A young child is often overwhelmed emotionally at these details.

Suggest a child paint or color a picture after he hears the Easter story. This art experience provides a way of seeing what was most important in the story from his perspective. After he has drawn or painted whatever he wants, talk with him about his art. If he has any negative feelings, these feelings will probably come to light in the conversation about his painting. After hearing the Easter story, a child may ask, "Where is Jesus now?" "Jesus is in heaven," is usually easily accepted by the questioning child. His reaction to this information, however, depends on his concept of heaven and of God. If the child understands heaven as a happy place where God and the Lord Jesus are, where no one is sick, or hurt, then his feelings will likely be positive.

Guiding the young child toward Jesus

The adult who wants to help a child toward God, rather than hinder him, has the responsibility to ask questions that will show the degree of understanding the child has about salvation, plus the level of commitment he has to that belief. For this reason, adults should avoid asking leading questions that put words in the child's mouth, also those questions that can be answered yes or no.

Five-year-old Jason's father was very pleased when his son announced, "Daddy, I want Jesus to come into my heart."

He responded by saying, "I'm very happy that you are thinking about this, Jason, because it is the most important decision you will ever make in your life. Tell me, what do you like most about Jesus?"

This question was less threatening than a straight, "Why do you want to become a Christian?" and thus was easier for Jason to answer. Also, his father hoped it would reveal some of Jason's thoughts and emotions about the Lord.

"I guess I like the way He fed all those people with the boy's lunch," was Jason's reply.

"That was one way He showed people that He loved them," said Dad. "Tell me some other things you like about Him."

Jason mentioned several other events from the life of Jesus, and finally mentioned that he liked Jesus because He loved everybody.

"That's a good answer, Jason. I love Jesus very much, because I know that He loves me."

"I love Jesus, too," said Jason.

"Let's tell Jesus that we love Him." Following very simple prayers by father and son, Dad asked, "Jason, do you want to talk about this some more right now, or do you want to do it tonight at bedtime?" Jason had had enough for one session, and ran outside. As Dad thought about their conversation, he noted that Jason had not expressed any awareness of how Jesus related personally to him, other than that He loved him.

That night, Dad asked Jason, "Do you remember what we said about Jesus this afternoon? Do you want to talk about Him some more?" Jason did. Then Dad said, "We talked today about loving Jesus. Tell me what people do when they love someone very much."

Jason thought. "They do kind things. They want to make them happy."

"That's right, Jason. Now tell me what happens if someone does something to a person they love that makes them unhappy."

"You have to say you're sorry," was Jason's reply.

"Tell me what it means to be sorry," Dad continued.

"Sorry means you are sad you did something, and won't do it again," Jason said.

Dad looked straight into Jason's eyes. "Now I'm going to ask you a hard question. Have you ever done anything that made Jesus unhappy?"

This question led Jason to confession of several acts that he felt were wrong. It was an easy step here to lead Jason to a prayer in which he said he was sorry for what he had done wrong.

"Jason, Jesus loves you very much, even when you do something bad. But, I am sure He is very happy because you have told Him you are sorry for those things. Let's talk about this again in a few days."

By this time Jason had indicated that he knew the difference between right and wrong, and had an awareness of the effects of his actions. More important, he seemed anxious to do the right thing instead of the wrong.

At the next conversation on the subject, Jason's dad asked him, "Why do people need to become part of God's family?" Jason was stymied here, so his dad explained to him how God wanted to help people to be able to do right things instead of wrong things. He raised the question again several days later. Jason explained in his five-year-old vocabulary his need for forgiveness. To be sure that Jason was not just repeating words he had heard, his dad phrased the question differently. "Tell me what happens to someone who asks to become part of God's family." Then, "Tell me how you can become part of God's family." Again, this required some help from Dad in getting the answers stated, and again the subject was held over until another day.

Each time the two discussed the question, the father was careful to ask Jason if he wanted to talk about it. If not, assurance was given that anytime Jason wanted to, Dad would be willing. Also, whenever Jason used a theological term, such as "saved," "forgiven," or "into my heart," Dad would ask Jason to explain what the word meant. Whenever Dad felt he needed to clarify an idea for Jason, that idea would be brought up again in the next conversation to see if Jason really understood.

The day that Jason and his dad finally knelt down and Jason specifically asked Jesus to forgive him for his sin and to become a member of God's family was certainly memorable. But it was not the first time they had prayed about such things. Nor was it the last; for Jason's father was equally concerned with nurturing Jason's growing understandings about being a Christian as he had been in helping Jason to make his own, clearly understood commitment to Jesus Christ.

Notes

1. F. W. Eastman, "Children's Questions and Comments About the Christian Faith," in *Religious Education,* 1963, vol. 58, p. 549.
2. Zimmerman, *Doctrine for 3's to 5's,* p. 103.
3. John Krahn, "Death and the Five- and Six-Year-Old," in *Lutheran Education,* 1973, September, pp. 49-54.
4. Harrell and Haystead, *Creative Bible Learning for Young Children,* p. 132.

CHAPTER SEVEN

The Child and God

"Who made God?"

"Nobody made God. He has always been alive."

"But, how did He get borned?"

"God isn't like us. He didn't have to be born. He has always been alive."

"But, . . . but, . . . but, who made Him?"

"This is very hard to understand, isn't it? There are many things about God I don't understand yet. All I know is that God was alive before anything else."

"But how did He get Hisself?"

Trying to answer the persistent questions of a child can often exhaust an adult's resources. Most children have more questions than adults have answers, especially when the subject is God. There is probably no concept that challenges the limits of human intelligence and imagination any more than the idea of God. Every civilization of history has wrestled with the idea of God. The greatest minds of all time have struggled to understand the infinite.

How, then, can a young child, who is just being introduced to the reality of daily life, be expected to fathom such an immense concept? Why should anyone even mention God to a child whose limited experience virtually guarantees that he will misunderstand much of what he hears?

A child's eagerness to know about the things around him usually stimulates his thinking and questions. Out of his curiosity he begins to want to know where things come from. The birth of a baby, the growth of a flower, the warm sun, or chilling wind can all be the event that will stimulate a lifelong search for answers.

Adults who possess a Christian faith of any degree, and who often feel puzzled about ways to answer children's questions, sometimes find it easy to simply reply, "God made it." This seems to satisfy most young inquirers for the present.

Also, many parents want their children to begin learning about God as early as possible, so as to build a foundation for later Christian growth. In either case, the information the child receives about God will not be easily understood by the child. Because he cannot see or hear God, he will not have many direct experiences that help him to correct inaccurate concepts in many areas. In a great many cases the child arrives at an idea of what God is like very early in life and then has little reason to alter it in succeeding years. Without direct experience to modify or expand a level of understanding, the child is confined to a concept that does not mature with him. Many people who work with adolescents and young adults find that young people who turn away from Christianity are in reality rejecting their childish misconceptions of what God is.

The problem calls for a careful analysis of what children actually do think about God, how they develop their concepts, and ways of helping to prepare them for more mature understandings. A comment by an early childhood specialist may serve as a word of caution before approaching this task: Could it be possible that the angels snicker at our "mature" ideas of God in the same way we find the ideas of young children so naively amusing?

THE CHILD'S ATTITUDE ABOUT GOD

A child's attitude is far more significant and enduring than his level of understanding information. Errors in knowledge can be corrected easier than negative feelings can be changed. Obviously, the two areas are closely related and each has an influence upon the other. However, early in life the extreme limits of the child's reasoning abilities make emotional qualities more vital than at other stages of his development.

When the child thinks about God, his understanding may be immature and even contradictory. But his feelings about God are usually quite definite. Some children learn very young to fear God as a powerful judge who will punish them for any wrongdoing. Others learn to associate God with all the good experiences of their life and consider Him a helpful friend, concerned with their well-being. Almost all children regard Him with a great deal of awe and wonder, and a certain degree of nervous uncertainty. In spite of what a particular child may say about God's actions, a basic emotional tone will underlie the surface beliefs, sometimes with a totally opposite meaning.[1]

The child's underlying attitude toward God is primarily formed in the process of interacting with adults, especially parents. (See chapter 3.) While God is always seen as more powerful than Dad and Mom, the kind of relationship the child has with his parents dominates his impressions of God. As the child's thinking matures, he gradually begins to transfer his feelings about parental omnipotence onto his idea of God.[2]

Thus, the child who is consistently disciplined by threats, yelling, and physical punishment will begin to think of God as angry and vengeful. Parents who regularly lose their tempers with their children build an image of God as irritable. A string of broken promises, inconsistent standards, and hypocritical morality leave the child with a concept on an unreliable God. Expressions of love, respect for the child's interest, consistent and reasonable discipline, and ethical behavior all combine to provide a positive base for a healthy, God concept. The inevitable misunderstandings about God can be minimized, or at least survived, if the child has this solid, wholesome environment to shape his attitudes.

THE CHILD'S THOUGHTS ABOUT GOD

A distinguishing feature of children's ideas of God is the almost universal view of Him in a somewhat human form. While recognizing His great power, children consistently picture God as an old man in flowing robes, with a long white beard, "longer than Santa Claus'." A great deal of childish imagination is evident in any collection of children's descriptions of God, whether verbal or pictorial. He may be the strongest of men, or even greater than any man could be. But He is still, in the final analysis, a physical being with all of the characteristics of men.[3]

While the child will say that everything God does is good, certain actions of God are sometimes seen as somewhat suspect. Children seem to believe that God is like adults who often do very strange things for no apparent reason, even though the child is told parents know what is best. Children may accept that dictum at face value. However, they will vigorously object in certain specific situations when adult behavior does not fit the best plan of action as viewed by the child.

Part of this problem is the difficulty the child has in acknowledging another person's point of view. He will frequently read his own motivations into a description of God's actions. Very logically he will conclude that God acts in a manner very similar to his own childish behavior. References to God's anger are interpreted in terms of childish behavior, such as becoming upset and angry. Thus, from a child's perspective, God changes His mind, makes mistakes, and all at the same time the child affirms belief in God's protection.[4]

Many children seem to understand the concept of God's omnipresence, which is usually a comfort in times of stress. But the concept is so dominated by the child's reliance on physical qualities that the results are often somewhat ludicrous. "Is God really right here with us? Is He hiding behind the curtains? Is He in my pockets?" The nonphysical nature of God baffles the child.

The literal quality of a child's thinking creates problems

in understanding of God's use of His power. They often see Him utilizing His "hands" and "arms" or applying levitation in a manner similar to a magician. They expect God to work on external situations. For example, one boy interpreted the idea of God's care to mean that when he crossed the street God would stop the cars from hitting him.

Children also seem thoroughly convinced that God loves everyone. However, in a specific situation they may very easily affirm that one individual or group is more favored than another. In many Bible stories, it appears to a child the "heroes" deserve love more than the "villains." In everyday life, for example, a child really is convinced that he and his friends are special in God's sight.

Again, a young child's limited view of life hems him into only one perspective. Even when he may earnestly declare that God loves boys and girls in other countries equally with himself, he may act differently. The child's words are again an inaccurate gauge of his true feelings.

Heaven also comes in for its share of childish imaginings. To the child it is a physical place, located somewhere in the sky, often in or above the clouds. For some children it is a vague and misty abode for that strange man, God. Others conjure delightful visions of a spectacular playground where children are free to do everything they want. Heaven's desirabilities are not usually sufficient to make the child really want to go there. But it does serve as a useful catchall to locate any departed pets or relatives.[5]

In most Christian homes God is not an integral part of the child's day-by-day experiences. Except for meal and bedtime prayers and an occasional Bible story, He is comfortably removed from the life of the child. Unfortunately, many parents do not relate God to the important moments of their own lives. The child himself is too dominated by his immediate perceptions to be overly concerned with a God he has never seen.

ACTIVITIES FOR LEARNING ABOUT GOD

The effect of love and discipline

Adults who desire to provide children with positive models for their concepts of God should give special attention to two areas of their relationship with the child: love and discipline. The vast majority of adults who work closely with children claim to love them. However, the adult's profession of love is not the issue. The point is, does the child really feel that he is loved? Love for him consists of adults noticing him and the things that interest him. Love for the young child is usually very physical. Cuddling and patting are important for both boys and girls. Love also needs to be verbal. Words spoken at those times when the child is being physically loved reinforce the actions. Expressions of love need to be independent of a child's behavior. Love that must be earned is far too fragile a thing for any child to depend on. For if it can be earned, it can also be lost. A child's fear of losing someone's love creates tension, not assurance.

Discipline, which encompasses far more than punishment, is the process of molding attitudes and behavior in a careful and loving manner. Harsh or inconsistent methods, even with the best of intentions, result in frustration. Proper discipline is firm, but patient.

Unfortunately, God is often introduced into discipline of young children as a threat—a sad mistake indeed! The parent who must resort to threats is revealing his own weakness to the child.[6] This kind of discipline diminishes the respect the child has for the adult. In contrast, when adults offer guidelines that are reasonable and logical, the child develops his ability to make wise choices. Also, the child's view of the adult as guide and helper is strengthened. Using God as a threat is also unwise because the child will likely develop negative feelings towards God. These feelings often linger long after the specific incident has been long forgotten.

Relating God to child's experience

To help the child recognize God's presence and interest in everyday experiences, it is necessary to introduce God into conversations while the child is in the midst of a specific activity. The child who is sitting passively in a chair in Sunday School will not comprehend the teacher's assurances that God will help him to be good during the week. Both the child's difficulty in transferring learning from one situation to another, as well as the distance in both space and time from the actual situation, will leave the child with only vague and often fanciful ideas about what the teacher meant. From that standpoint, little Aaron was perfectly logical in blaming God for his misbehavior one day. "I asked God to help me be good, so it's His fault that I talked back to Mommy!"

Fortunately, Aaron's mother recognized that her son was not guilty of blasphemy, but was simply coming to a very logical conclusion from the limited information he had been given. She tried to help him correct his thinking by saying, "Aaron, God won't make us do anything. But I have found that when I really want to do the right thing, asking God to help me do it makes it easier. If I want to do something bad, God won't make me do something else."

This conversation with Aaron, in the middle of a very real encounter, helped him to clarify the concept. While there can be no firm assurance that he fully grasped his mother's meaning, he is closer to it than he would have been if the same information was handed to him apart from the specific situation. Even more important, Aaron's mother is establishing a pattern of answering his questions and responding to his statements. Giving attention to a child's interests strengthens parent/child relationships.

Michelle's father frequently took her to a nearby park where they enjoyed many activities. Frequent opportunities to mention God in very natural and specific ways occurred during these excursions. One day while looking at the park's rose garden in full bloom, her father asked, "Michelle, what would you think if there were no such things as flowers?"

"Then the park wouldn't be pretty," she answered.

"And what if there weren't any flowers anywhere?"

"I wouldn't like that. I think flowers are nice."

"So do I," said Father. "Aren't we glad God made these pretty flowers for us to enjoy!"

On another occasion, Michelle asked, "Did God make the swings and the slide?"

"What do you think?"

Michelle thought a moment, then answered, "I think some men made them."

"You're right. When God first made the world, He made people so they could think and plan and work. God knew that we would need to build houses and other buildings. And I think He knew that little girls would like to play on swings and slides."

The child's questions are one of the best indicators of the level of his thinking. The kinds of questions he asks assist adults in knowing how much information about God is appropriate at the time. The problem that most adults face is in determining if their answer was adequate. Again, the child's queries and comments are usually a good barometer.

Many teachers do as Michelle's father did, and respond to a question with a question. Guiding the child to think about his own inquiry can help both parent and child to think more clearly about the problem at hand. Another helpful approach is to follow an answer with a question to see how the child reacted to the new information.

After Mrs. Andrews would answer a question from her kindergartners, she would often ask, "What do you think of that?" She wisely sought to use her answers to stimulate further thought.

Questions and answers about God

What do you say to a child's questions about so complex a concept as God? For the answers to be meaningful, they must fit the specific child's present level of understanding. They must also fit the adult who is answering. For example, the adult who is cold and distant will probably have little success in explaining to a child how God loves that child. A loving and understanding adult might speak the same words. But the impact that answer would have on the child would be entirely different. The attitude of the adult makes the difference. In any case, the answer should make sense to the adult and not just be an attempt to parrot what he thinks is the "right" answer.

The latter approach can only make the discussion about God very hypocritical. The child is bound to discover the discrepancy sooner or later. It is far preferable to say, "I don't know. There are many things about God that nobody really knows." One father responded to a knotty question with, "I just don't know how to answer that. It's a good question, but I'm going to have to think about it for a few days. I might even ask someone else. But I'll sure try to find the answer for you."

"What does God look like?" is a common question asked by children. One teacher answered this way, "No one has ever seen God, so we don't know what He looks like. The Bible does talk about Him sometimes as if He looks like a man to help us be able to think about Him."

"Where does God live?" is another frequent query. A possible answer is, "God is everywhere, all at the same time. No one understands how He does that, but we know it is true." That answer may not satisfy the child, but it is preferable to locating God in a faraway "heaven." Also, leaving the child with the reality of mystery provides a means for avoiding simplistic answers that become locked in as he grows older.

"Where is heaven?" is similar to the previous question. The child hears the term used in sentences as a place name and assumes it is a physical location. Because the young child cannot comprehend the nonphysical, this is a question that drives parents to seek help from the "experts," or to seek refuge in a simple answer, "It's up in the sky." That answer runs into problems, however, when the child takes an airplane ride or watches rocket launchings on television. One parent preferred to answer like this, "Heaven is real, but no one has ever seen it. The Bible tells us that heaven is wonderful. But heaven is so different from anything we know that it's hard for us to understand what it's like." This does not free the child from his physical conceptualization, but at least it removes heaven from the path of a "747." One teacher's answer to a child who wondered when he would go to heaven was, "I don't know. It's not time yet for that to happen."

"How does God take care of me?" is the subject of an infinite variety of questions that relate to the kind and extent of influence God has in the child's life. The best answers focus the child's attention on the specific provisions God has provided for human sustenance. "God made the world with all the plants and animals we would need for food, clothes, and to build our houses. And He planned for people to have strong bodies so they can use these things that He made for us. And He planned for us to have families and friends so we could help each other." This kind of emphasis helps the child to appreciate his own abilities as God-given, and to be grateful for the people who are part of his life. It also helps the child to avoid the fanciful view that God protects by magical means, removing responsibility from the individual.

"Does God get mad?" is the type of question that involves God's response to the child's action. The child's interpretation of anger is totally conditioned by the expressions of it that he experienced in his interactions with other people. One of the nicest answers was given by

Andrea's grandmother. "God loves you so much, Andrea, that He always wants you to do what is best so you will be happy and make everyone else happy. When you do something that isn't the best, God is sad, for He knows you won't really be happy."

Notes

1. Goldman, *Religious Thinking from Childhood to Adolescence*, p. 140.
2. Piaget, *The Child's Conception of the World*, p. 354.
3. Ibid., p. 382.
4. Goldman, *Religious Thinking from Childhood to Adolescence*, p. 126.
5. Ibid., p. 89.
6. C. A. Nunve, "Child Control Through a 'Coalition with God,' " in *Child Development*, 1964, vol. 35, p. 417.

EPILOGUE

Learning That Makes a Difference

"What did you learn in Sunday School this morning, Eugene?"

(Silence.)

"What was the Bible story your teacher told?"

"I don't remember."

"Do you remember anything that happened?"

(Silence.)

"You know, Eugene, your teacher told me that you were just full of wiggles this morning. Did you have a hard time sitting still?"

"Yes."

"Eugene, no wonder you didn't learn anything. You know we bring you to Sunday School to learn about God."

"But my teacher made me stay in my chair, and she teached, and teached, and I got so tired I just couldn't learn anything!"

Learning is a full-time job for young children. Everything in their world is so new and interesting that they continually feel a compulsion to explore and experiment. Within the first six years of life the child learns to control his physical functions, to coordinate his muscular endowment, to fluently speak the language of his parents, to react in his own unique style to a multitude of situations, and to interact effectively with other people. Quite an accomplishment for a young child! He possesses opinions, feelings, beliefs and information on a wide range of subjects. He has developed a personality structure that identifies him as a unique person.

Considering that knowledge at his birth is zero, the quantity and quality of learning that a child accumulates in six years is truly remarkable. It is especially remarkable when we recognize that the director of this learning process is primarily the child himself. He learns the things he experiences in his environment. His interests, abilities and attention span are the dominant factors in the maze of his experiences. While parents and peers provided many of the ingredients for these experiences, the child sets his pace for his learning program.[1] He applies this same kind of learning technique in the area of his spiritual development. He will take from every conversation, song, story, and lesson only those aspects that are at his level of comprehension and interest, regardless of adult intentions.

PRINCIPLES FOR GUIDING SPIRITUAL DEVELOPMENT

A Sunday School teacher was seeking to impress her

five-year-olds with the significance of the Ten Commandments. As the children grew increasingly restless, she patiently explained each of the concepts involved. Realizing that her young charges did not seem to be appreciating the great truths she was sharing, she asked, "If you were asked to make up ten commandments that would help everyone be happy and live together the right way, what would you think would be most important?" Gregory came to life. "Thou shalt have fun," he declared firmly.

Theologians might dispute Gregory's commandment. Although he may not know theology, he certainly knows children. The vast majority of the miscellaneous, but essential, learning that the child accomplishes depends to a large extent on his enjoyment of the learning task.[2] No child would learn to talk if he did not see the ability to communicate as very desirable. Why do all normal babies exert themselves to roll over, sit up, crawl and finally walk? For them there is great satisfaction in seeing the world from a new perspective. Each child gains a splendid feeling of achievement in being able to do something new. And, of course, Mom and Dad get so excited about each new trick that the child becomes motivated to do things just to see adult reactions.

Unfortunately, much of the pure pleasure of learning goes out the window when people approach the child's Christian education. Suddenly, parents begin talking about things the child "ought to know," with no consideration about whether he "wants to know." Comments such as, "It's for his own good," and "He'll appreciate it when he's older," reflect adult thinking. Thus, the child's instruction takes on all the qualities of administering a dose of castor oil, often with the same kind of reaction by the child.

How can adults talk about faith as the essential ingredient of a happy satisfying life, then make the teaching of it to children an endurance contest? How can anyone justify boring children with the Bible? If Christianity is to be enriching, then the teaching of it must take on the qualities of delight and joy for the child. The method must fit the objective.

Relationships

The most effective method for teaching Christian concepts to a young child is for a positive relationship to exist between that child and adults who have a faith that makes a difference in the quality of their lives. Each of the concepts considered in this book is more effectively communicated to a child through the relationships the child experiences than through any verbal expressions.[3]

The attitude of the child under six is of far greater consequence than his factual knowledge. The development of positive feelings and values should be of much greater concern to parents and teachers than the child's ability to recite verses or recount information. Surrounding the child with secure and loving relationships with understanding Christians is the best method anyone can use.

Thought depends on action

Those who guide a child's spiritual development need to keep in mind that the child's thought processes are dependent upon accompanying action.[4] The child does not reason independent of real-life experiences that call into play his physical senses. Simply talking about Christian ways of living, for example, does not provide the child with ample input for him to develop valid, realistic concepts. He needs repeated and varied opportunities to put Bible truths into action—to feel what it's like to be a giver as well as a receiver.

Parents have innumerable opportunities during the course of daily activities to allow their own values to become evident to the child. These everyday experiences provide material for meaningful conversations. Teachers who work with children in the more artificial setting of a classroom need to plan specific opportunities and create situations in which the child can learn through firsthand experiences.

Response to children's questions

Allow a child's questions to guide the direction and level of his learning situations. Far too often adults attempt to organize information logically, presenting an orderly outline of subject matter. However, the young child's learning should be structured psychologically, moving with the ever-changing interests of the child.[5]

Frequently Jesus used this method by tailoring His discussions to the questions asked by His listeners. Even the New Testament epistles were not written as step-by-step essays on religion. They were written in response to real questions and real problems that were being raised in the young churches of the apostolic age.

A child proceeds with learning in much the same way—asking questions to help solve current problems. He does not wait to learn a new word until he has completely mastered an easier one. Nor does he wait until he has succeeded with walking before starting on another skill. He works on whatever is at hand, whatever appears of interest. As a result he learns many things in what appears to be a highly unorganized approach. His learning might not be systematic, but it works for him.

Adults need to give the child exposure to many situations, stimulate his interest and his questions, and then to answer those questions in ways to further spark his thinking. Avoid the desire to follow up the child's question with complete coverage of the subject at hand. Rather, develop the skill of sensing the amount of interest the child has at the moment and satisfy only that much.

Repetition

Repetition is an essential ingredient in a child's learning process. When an activity is fun for a child, his watchword is, "Do it again." He needs opportunities to repeat his learning in a variety of ways. For example, when a kindergartner teacher is presenting a unit of lessons involving the concept of sharing, she will provide learning activities—firsthand experiences—that encourage sharing: her pictures will illustrate sharing situations; her conversation will focus on that concept as she reinforces acceptable behavior. "Share what you have with others" (1 Tim. 6:18, *TLB*), might be the Bible verse she uses as she guides children's thoughts and words.

Adults often tire of the simplicity of many childish games and interests by focusing merely on the content. However, when an adult can sense the wonder in the child's eyes, and feel the joy of insight and discovery, then the learning of the child becomes one of life's most rewarding opportunities for adult renewal. The adult who seeks to teach a child soon finds that he has learned more from the child than he has taught.

Molding a young child's knowledge and attitude about God is truly an awesome responsibility. Jesus felt this strongly enough to declare that "whoever causes one of these little ones who believe in Me to stumble, it is better for him that a heavy millstone be hung around his neck, and that he be drowned in the depth of the sea" (Matt. 18:6).

Why such a stern warning? Is it because in guiding a child we have the future in our grasp? Is it because the young child is so trusting that he will confidently follow our guidance? Is it because children are in some way so important to God that He thus gives them this special concern?

Jesus followed His admonition with a powerful message of encouragement: "It is not the will of your Father who is in heaven that one of these little ones perish" (Matt. 18:14). Imagine! The person who is committed to nurturing the spiritual life of a child is working in cooperation with the will of God the Father!

Because God earnestly desires that children grow to love and worship Him, He offers all the help needed to anyone who shares His longing for the early guidance of little children. Whether you are a parent or a teacher, you can enjoy the extraordinary adventure of working in partnership with God!

God has made even the youngest child curious and ready to learn. What he learns and how you help him is up to you. And you can't begin too soon!

Notes

1. Munsinger, *Fundamentals of Child Development,* p. 124.
2. Ibid., p. 106.
3. Zimmerman, *Doctrine for 3's to 5's,* p. 7.
4. David Elkind, "The Origins of Religion in the Child," in *Review of Religious Research,* 1970, vol. 12, p. 36
5. R. S. Lee, *Your Growing Child and Religion* (New York: Macmillan, 1964), p. 160.

BIBLIOGRAPHY

For Further Reading

Ahlem, Lloyd. *Do I Have To Be Me?* Ventura, CA: Regal Books, 1973.

Armsby, R. E. "A Re-examination of the Development of Moral Judgment in Children." *Child Development,* 1971, vol. 42.

Briggs, Dorothy. *Your Child's Self-Esteem: The Key to His Life.* Garden City, NY: Doubleday, 1970.

Childers, P., and Wimmer, M. "The Concept of Death in Early Childhood." *Child Development,* 1971, vol. 42.

Cowles, M. "Four Views of Learning and Development." *Education Leadership,*1971, vol. 28.

Cox, E. "Honest to Goldman: An Assessment." *Religious Education,* 1968, vol. 63.

Dobson, James. *Hide or Seek.* Old Tappan, NJ: Fleming Revell, 1974.

Eastman, F. W. "Children's Questions and Comments About the Christian Faith." *Religious Education,* 1963, vol. 58.

Elkind, David. "The Origins of Religion in the Child." *Review of Religious Research,* 1970, vol. 12.

Erikson, Erik. *Childhood and Society,* 2nd ed. New York: W.W. Norton, 1963.

Ginsburg, Herbert, and Opper, Sylvia. *Piaget's Theory of Intellectual Development: An Introduction.* Englewood Cliffs, N.J.: Prentice-Hall, 1969.

Goldman, Ronald. *Readiness for Religion.* New York: Seabury Press, 1965.

Graebner, O. E. "Child Concepts of God." *Religious Education,* 1964, vol. 59.

Harrell, Donna, and Haystead, Wesley. *Creative Bible Learning for Young Children.* Ventura, CA: Regal Books, 1977.

Hendricks, William. *A Theology for Children.* Nashville: Broadman Press, 1980.

Kohlberg, Lawrence. "Development of Moral Character and Moral Ideology." In M. Hoffman and L. Hoffman (Eds.) *Review of Child Development Research,* vol. 1, New York: Russell Sage Foundation, 1964.

Krahn, John. "A Comparison of Kohlberg's and Piaget's Type I Morality." *Religious Education,* 1971, vol. 66.

Lawrence, P. J. "Children's Thinking About Religion: A Study of Concrete Operational Thinking." *Religious Education,* 1965, vol. 60.

Maslow, A. H. *Motivation and Personality.* New York: Harper and Row, 1954.

Miller, Keith. *The Becomers.* Waco, Texas: Word, 1973.

Munsinger, H. *Fundamentals of Child Development.* New York: Holt, Rinehart & Winston, 1971.

Nordberg, R. B. "Developing the Idea of God in Children." *Religious Education,* 1971, vol. 66.

O'Neill, R. P., and Donovan, M. A. *Children, Church and God: The Case Against Formal Religious Education.* New York: Corpus Books, 1970.

Piaget, Jean. *The Moral Judgment of the Child.* Glencoe, Illinois: Free Press, 1948.

______. *Origins of Intelligence.* New York: International Universities Press, 1964.

______. *Science of Education and the Psychology of the Child.* New York: Orion Press, 1970.

Sholl, D. "The Contributions of Lawrence Kohlberg to Religious and Moral Education." *Religious Education,* 1971, vol. 66.

Zimmerman, Eleanor. *Doctrine for 3's to 5's.* Philadelphia: Lutheran Church Press, 1963.